MICHEL ANGELO

Emery Walker Ph.Sc.

From the portrait in the possession of.
The Earl of Wemyss & March.

THE SONNETS OF
MICHAEL ANGELO
BUONARROTI

NOW FOR THE FIRST TIME TRANSLATED
INTO RHYMED ENGLISH BY

JOHN ADDINGTON SYMONDS

Χρύσεων χάλκεια

WITH A PORTRAIT

LONDON
JOHN MURRAY, ALBEMARLE STREET, W.

First Edition (Smith, Elder & Co.) *January*, 1878.
Third Impression   .   .   .   *July*, 1912.
Reprinted (John Murray)   .   . *January*, 1926.

PRINTED IN GREAT BRITAIN BY
WILLIAM CLOWES AND SONS, LIMITED, LONDON AND BECCLES.

TO

S. F. A.

PREFATORY NOTE

AFTER some deliberation, and at the risk of offending the sensibility of scholars, I have adopted the old English spelling of Michael Angelo's name, feeling that no orthographical accuracy can outweigh the associations implied in that familiar title. Michael Angelo has a place among the highest with Homer and Titian, with Virgil and Petrarch, with Raphael and Paul; nor do I imagine that any alteration for the better would be effected by substituting for these time-honoured names Homêros and Tiziano, Vergilius and Petrarca, Raffaello and Paulus.

I wish here to express my heartiest thanks to Signore V. de Tivoli for calling my attention to

PREFATORY NOTE

the sonnet of Michael Angelo deciphered by him
on the back of a drawing in the Taylor Gallery
at Oxford.

Portions both of the Introduction and the
Translations forming this volume, have already
appeared in the *Contemporary Review* and the
Cornhill Magazine.

DAVOS PLATZ :
Dec. 1877.

CONTENTS

INTRODUCTION

I

IT is with diffidence that I offer a translation of Michael Angelo's sonnets, for the first time completely rendered into English rhyme. My excuse, if I can plead any for so bold an attempt, may be found in this—that, so far as I am aware, no other English writer has dealt with Michael Angelo's verses since the publication of his autograph.

My translation of Michael Angelo's sonnets has been made from Signor Cesare Guasti's edition of the autograph, first given to the world in 1863.[1] This masterpiece of laborious and

[1] "Le Rime di Michelangelo Buonarroti, Pittore, Scultore e Architetto, cavate dagli Autografi e pubblicate da Cesare Guasti, Accademico della Crusca. In Firenze, per Felice le Monnier. M.DCCC.LXIII."

minute scholarship is based upon a collation of
the various manuscripts preserved in the Casa
Buonarroti at Florence with the Vatican and
other Codices. It adheres to the original ortho-
graphy of Michael Angelo, and omits no fragment
of his indubitable compositions.[1] Signor Guasti
prefaces the text he has so carefully prepared
with a discourse upon the poetry of Michael
Angelo and a description of the manuscripts.
To the poems themselves he adds a prose
paraphrase, and prints upon the same page
with each composition the version published by
Michelangelo Buonarroti in 1623.[2]

[1] See, however, page xlvii. of Signor Guasti's *Discorso*.

[2] I have so fully expressed my admiration for Signor
Guasti's edition in the text that I may allow myself to point
out in a note what seems to me its chief defect, and why I
think there is still, perhaps, room for another and more
critical edition. The materials are amply and conscien-
tiously supplied by Signor Guasti; indeed, I suppose we are
justified in believing that his single volume reproduces
all the extant manuscript authorities, with the exception,
perhaps, of the British Museum Codex. But, while it is so
comprehensive, we are still left in some doubt as to the
preference of one reading rather than another in the large
type text presented to us as the final version of each composition. It is true that when this was possible, Signor
Guasti invariably selected one of the autographs, that is,

INTRODUCTION

Before the publication of this volume, all studies of Michael Angelo's poetry, all translations made of it, and all hypotheses deduced from the sculptor's verse in explanation of his theory or his practice as an artist, were based upon the edition of 1623. It will not be super-

a copy in the poet's own handwriting. But when we consider that very frequently Michael Angelo's own autographs give twice as many various readings as there are lines in a sonnet, when we reflect that we do not always possess the copies which he finally addressed to his friends, and when, moreover, we find that their readings (*e.g.* those of the Riccio MS. and those cited by Varchi) differ considerably from Michael Angelo's rough copies, we must conclude that even the autographs do not invariably represent these poems in the final form which he adopted. There is therefore much room left for critical comparison and selection. We are, in fact, still somewhat in the same position as Michelangelo the younger. Whether any application of the critical method will enable us to do again successfully what he so clumsily attempted—that is, to reproduce a correct text from the *débris* offered to our selective faculty—I do not feel sure. Meanwhile I am quite certain that his principle was a wrong one, and that he dealt most unjustifiably with his materials. For this reason I cordially accept Signor Guasti's labours, with the reservation I have attempted to express in this note. They have indeed brought us far closer to Michael Angelo's real text, but we must be careful to remember that we have not even now arrived with certainty at what he would himself have printed if he had prepared his own edition for the press.

fluous to describe what that edition was, and how its text differed from that now given to the light, in order that the relation of my own English version to those which have preceded it may be rightly understood.[1]

Michael Angelo seems to have entertained no thought of printing his poems in his lifetime. He distributed them freely among his friends, of whom Sebastiano del Piombo, Luigi del Riccio, Donato Giannotti, Vittoria Colonna, and Tommaso de' Cavalieri were in this respect the most favoured. In course of time some of these friends, partly by the gift of the originals, and partly by obtaining copies, formed more or less complete collections; and it undoubtedly occurred to more than one to publish them. Ascanio Condivi, at the close of his biography, makes this announcement : " I hope ere long to make public some of his sonnets and madrigals, which I have been long collecting, both from himself

---

[1] As far as I am aware, no complete translation of Michael Angelo's sonnets has hitherto been made in English. The specimens produced by Southey, Wordsworth, Harford, Longfellow, and Mr. Taylor, moreover render Michelangelo's *rifacimento.*

and others who possessed them, with a view to proving to the world the force of his inventive genius and the beauty of the thoughts produced by that divine spirit." Condivi's promise was not fulfilled. With the exception of two or three pieces printed by Vasari, and the extracts quoted by Varchi in his *Lezione*,[1] the poems of Michael Angelo remained in manuscript for fifty-nine years after his death. The most voluminous collection formed part of the Buonarroti archives ; but a large quantity preserved by Luigi del Riccio, and from him transferred to Fulvio Orsini, had passed into the Vatican Library, when Michelangelo the younger conceived the plan of publishing his grand-uncle's poetry. Michelangelo obtained leave to transcribe the Vatican MSS. with his own hand ; and after taking pains to collate all the autographs and copies in existence, he set himself to compare their readings, and to form

---

[1] " Lezione di Benedetto Varchi sopra il sottoscritto Sonetto di Michelagnolo Buonarroti, fatta da lui pubblicamente nella Accademia Fiorentina la Seconda Domenica di Quaresima l'anno MDXLVI." The sonnet commented by Varchi is Guasti's No. xv.

a final text for publication. Here, however, began what we may call the Tragedy of his Rifacimento. The more he studied his great ancestor's verses, the less he liked or dared to edit them unaltered. Some of them expressed thoughts and sentiments offensive to the Church. In some the Florentine patriot spoke over-boldly. Others exposed their author to misconstruction on the score of personal morality.[1] All were ungrammatical, rude in versification, crabbed and obscure in thought—the rough-hewn blockings-out of poems rather than finished works of art, as it appeared to the scrupulous, decorous, elegant, and timorous Academician of a feebler age. While pondering these difficulties, and

[1] I have elsewhere recorded my disagreement with Signor Guasti and Signor Gotti, and my reasons for thinking that Varchi and Michelangelo the younger were right in assuming that the sonnets addressed to Tommaso de' Cavalieri (especially xxx., xxxi., lii.) expressed the poet's admiration for masculine beauty. See "Renaissance in Italy, Fine Arts," pp. 521, 522. At the same time, though I agree with Buonarroti's first editor in believing that a few of the sonnets "risguardano, come si conosce chiaramente, amor platonico virile," I quite admit—as what student of early Italian poetry will not admit ?—that a woman is generally intended under the title of "Signore" and "amico."

comparing the readings of his many manuscripts, the thought occurred to Michelangelo that, between leaving the poems unpublished and printing them in all their rugged boldness, lay the middle course of reducing them to smoothness of diction, lucidity of meaning, and propriety of sentiment.[1] In other words, he began, as Signor Guasti pithily describes his method, " to change halves of lines, whole verses, ideas : if he found a fragment, he completed it : if brevity involved the thought in obscurity, he amplified : if the obscurity seemed incurable, he amputated : for superabundant wealth of conception he substituted vacuity ; smoothed asperities ; softened salient lights." The result was that a medley of garbled phrases, additions, alterations, and sophistications was foisted on the world as the veritable product of the mighty sculptor's genius. That Michelangelo meant well to his illustrious ancestor is certain. That he took the greatest pains in executing his ungrateful and disastrous

---

[1] *Ridurle* is his own phrase. He also speaks of *trasmutare* and *risoluzione* to explain the changes he effected.

task is no less clear.[1]   But the net result of his meddlesome benevolence has been that now for two centuries and a half the greatest genius of the Italian Renaissance has worn the ill-fitting disguise prepared for him by a literary " breeches-maker." In fact, Michael Angelo the poet suffered no less from his grand-nephew than Michael Angelo the fresco painter from his follower Daniele da Volterra.

Nearly all Michael Angelo's sonnets express personal feelings, and by far the greater number of them were composed after his sixtieth year. To whom they were addressed, we only know in a few instances. Vittoria Colonna and Tommaso de' Cavalieri, the two most intimate friends of his old age in Rome, received from him some of the most pathetically beautiful of his love-poems. But to suppose that either the one or the other was the object of more than a few well-authenticated sonnets would be hazardous. Nothing is more clear than that Michael Angelo worshipped Beauty in the Platonic spirit, passing beyond its personal and specific manifestations to the

[1] See Guasti's *Discorso*, p. xliv.

universal and impersonal. This thought is repeated over and over again in his poetry ; and if we bear in mind that he habitually regarded the loveliness of man or woman as a sign and symbol of eternal and immutable beauty, we shall feel it of less importance to discover who it was that prompted him to this or that poetic utterance. That the loves of his youth were not so tranquil as those of his old age, appears not only from the regrets expressed in his religious verses, but also from one or two of the rare sonnets referable to his manhood.

The love of beauty, the love of Florence, and the love of Christ, are the three main motives of his poetry. This is not the place to discuss at length the nature of his philosophy, his patriotism, or his religion ; to enquire how far he retained the early teaching of Ficino and Savonarola ; or to trace the influence of Dante and the Bible on his mind. I may, however, refer my readers who are interested in these questions, to the Discourse of Signor Guasti, the learned essay of Mr. J. E. Taylor, and the refined study of Mr. W. H. Pater. My own views will be found expressed in the third volume of my " Renaissance in Italy "; and where I think it necessary, I shall take occasion to repeat them in the notes appended to my translation.

THE SONNETS
OF MICHAEL ANGELO
BUONARROTI

I

PER DANTE ALIGHIERI
[1545]

Dal ciel discese, e col mortal suo, poi
  Che visto ebbe l'inferno giusto e 'l pio,
  Ritornò vivo a contemplare Dio,
  Per dar di tutto il vero lume a noi :
Lucente stella, che co' raggi suoi
  Fe chiaro, a torto, el nido ove naqqu' io ;
  Nè sare' 'l premio tutto 'l mondo rio :
  Tu sol, che la creasti, esser quel puoi.
Di Dante dico, che mal conosciute
  Fur l' opre suo da quel popolo ingrato,
  Che solo a' iusti manca di salute.
Fuss' io pur lui ! c' a tal fortuna nato,
  Per l' aspro esilio suo, con la virtute,
  Dare' del mondo il più felice stato.

2

I

ON DANTE ALIGHIERI

FROM heaven his spirit came, and robed in clay
    The realms of justice and of mercy trod,
    Then rose a living man to gaze on God,
    That he might make the truth as clear as day.
For that pure star that brightened with his ray
    The undeserving nest where I was born,
    The whole wide world would be a prize to scorn ;
    None but his Maker can due guerdon pay.
I speak of Dante, whose high work remains
    Unknown, unhonoured by that thankless brood
    Who only to just men deny their wage.
Were I but he !   Born for like lingering pains,
    Against his exile coupled with his good
    I'd gladly change the world's best heritage !

II

PER IL MEDESIMO

Quante dirne si de' non si può dire,
    Chè troppo agli orbi il suo splendor s' accese :
    Biasmar si può più 'l popol che l' offese,
    C' al suo men pregio ogni maggior salire.
Questo discese a' merti del fallire,
    Per l' util nostro, e poi a Dio ascese :
    E le porte che 'l ciel non gli contese,
    La patria chiuse al suo giusto desire.
Ingrata, dico, e della suo fortuna
    A suo danno nutrice ; ond' è ben segnio,
    C' a' più perfetti abonda di più guai.
Fra mille altre ragion sol ha quest' una :
    Se par non ebbe il suo esilio indegnio,
    Simil uom nè maggior non nacque mai.

II

ON DANTE ALIGHIERI

No tongue can tell of him what should be told,
    For on blind eyes his splendour shines too strong ;
      'Twere easier to blame those who wrought him
        wrong,
    Than sound his least praise with a mouth of gold.
He to explore the place of pain was bold,
    Then soared to God, to teach our souls by song ;
    The gates heaven oped to bear his feet along,
    Against his just desire his country rolled.
Thankless I call her, and to her own pain
    The nurse of fell mischance ; for sign take this,
    That ever to the best she deals more scorn :
Among a thousand proofs let one remain ;
    Though ne'er was fortune more unjust than his,
    His equal or his better ne'er was born.

III

A PAPA GIULIO II.
[1506]

Signor, se vero è alcun proverbio antico,
    Questo è ben quel, che Chi può, mai non vuole.
    Tu hai creduto a favole e parole,
    E premiato chi è del ver nimico.
Io sono, e fui già tuo buon servo antico ;
    A te son dato come i raggi al sole ;
    E del mio tempo non t' incresce o duole,
    E men ti piaccio se più m' affatico.
Già sperai ascender per la tua altezza ;
    E 'l giusto peso, e la potente spada
    Fassi al bisogno, e non la voce d' Ecco.
Ma 'l cielo è quel ch' ogni virtù disprezza
    Locarla al mondo, se vuol ch' altri vada
    A prender frutto d' un arbor ch' è secco.

III

TO POPE JULIUS II.

My Lord ! if ever ancient saw spake sooth,
    Hear this which saith : Who can, doth never will.
    Lo ! thou hast lent thine ear to fables still,
    Rewarding those who hate the name of truth.
I am thy drudge and have been from my youth—
    Thine, like the rays which the sun's circle fill ;
    Yet of my dear time's waste thou think'st no ill :
    The more I toil, the less I move thy ruth.
Once 'twas my hope to raise me by thy height ;
    But 'tis the balance and the powerful sword
    Of Justice, not false Echo, that we need.
Heaven, as it seems, plants virtue in despite
    Here on the earth, if this be our reward—
    To seek for fruit on trees too dry to breed.

IV

QUA si fa elmi di calici e spade,
  E 'l sangue di Cristo si vend' a giumelle,
  E croce e spine son lance e rotelle ;
  E pur da Cristo pazienzia cade !
Ma non c' arivi più 'n queste contrade,
  Chè n' andre' 'l sangue suo 'nsin alle stelle,
  Poscia che a Roma gli vendon la pelle ;
  E èci d' ogni ben chiuso le strade.
S' i' ebbi ma' voglia a posseder tesauro,
  Per ciò che qua opra da me è partita,
  Può quel nel manto che Medusa in Mauro.
Ma se alto in cielo è povertà gradita,
  Qual fia di nostro stato il gran restauro,
  S' un altro segno amorza l' altra vita ?

IV

ON ROME IN THE PONTIFICATE
OF JULIUS II.

HERE helms and swords are made of chalices :
    The blood of Christ is sold so much the quart :
    His cross and thorns are spears and shields ;
        and short
    Must be the time ere even his patience cease.
Nay let him come no more to raise the fees
    Of this foul sacrilege beyond report !
    For Rome still flays and sells him at the court,
    Where paths are closed to virtue's fair increase.
Now were fit time for me to scrape a treasure !
    Seeing that work and gain are gone ; while he
    Who wears the robe, is my Medusa still.
God welcomes poverty perchance with pleasure :
    But of that better life what hope have we,
    When the blessed banner leads to nought but ill ?

V

A GIOVANNI DA PISTOIA

Quando l' Autore Dipingeva la Volta Della Sistina

[1509]

I' ho già fatto un gozzo in questo stento,
    Come fa l' acqua a' gatti in Lombardia,
    O ver d' altro paese che si sia,
    Ch' a forza 'l ventre appicca sotto 'l mento.
La barba al cielo, e la memoria sento
    In sullo scrignio, e 'l petto fo d' arpia ;
    E 'l pennel sopra 'l viso tuttavia
    Mel fa, gocciando, un ricco pavimento.
E lombi entrati mi son nella peccia,
    E fo del cul per contrapeso groppa,
    E' passi senza gli occhi muovo invano.
Dinanzi mi s' allunga la corteccia,
    E per piegarsi adietro si ragroppa,
    E tendomi com' arco sorïano.
            Però fallace e strano
Surgie il iudizio che la mente porta ;
Chè mal si tra' per cerbottana torta.
            La mia pittura morta
Difendi orma', Giovanni, e 'l mio onore,
Non sendo in loco bon, nè io pittore.

6

V

ON THE PAINTING OF THE SISTINE CHAPEL

I've grown a goitre by dwelling in this den—
    As cats from stagnant streams in Lombardy,
    Or in what other land they hap to be—
    Which drives the belly close beneath the chin :
My beard turns up to heaven ; my nape falls in,
    Fixed on my spine : my breast-bone visibly
    Grows like a harp : a rich embroidery
    Bedews my face from brush-drops thick and thin.
My loins into my paunch like levers grind :
    My buttock like a crupper bears my weight ;
    My feet unguided wander to and fro ;
In front my skin grows loose and long ; behind,
    By bending it becomes more taut and strait ;
    Crosswise I strain me like a Syrian bow :
      Whence false and quaint, I know,
    Must be the fruit of squinting brain and eye ;
    For ill can aim the gun that bends awry.
      Come then, Giovanni, try
    To succour my dead pictures and my fame ;
    Since foul I fare and painting is my shame.

VI

CONTRO A' PISTOIESI

I' l' ho, vostra mercè, per ricevuto,
 E hollo letto delle volte venti.
 Tal pro vi facci alla natura i denti,
  Co' 'l cibo al corpo quando gli è pasciuto.
I' ho pur, poi ch' i' vi lasciai, saputo
 Che Cain fu de' vostri anticedenti :
 Nè voi da quel tralignate altrimenti ;
  Chè s' altri ha ben, vel pare aver perduto.
Invidiosi, superbi, al ciel nimici ;
 La carità del prossimo v' è a noia,
 E sol del vostro danno siete amici.
Se dice il Poeta, di Pistoia,
 Istieti a mente, e basta : e se tu dici
 Ben di Fiorenza, tu mi dai la soia,
    Qual prezïosa gioia
 È certo : ma per te non già s'intende ;
 Perchè poca virtù non la comprende.

VI

INVECTIVE AGAINST THE PEOPLE OF PISTOJA

I'VE gotten it, thanks to your courtesy ;
    And I have read it twenty times or so :
    Thus much may your sharp snarling profit you,
    As food our flesh filled to satiety.
After I left you, I could plainly see
    How Cain was of your ancestors : I know
    You do not shame his lineage, for lo,
    Your brother's good still seems your injury.
Envious you are, and proud, and foes to heaven ;
    Love of your neighbour still you loathe and hate,
    And only seek what must your ruin be.
If to Pistoja Dante's curse was given,
    Bear that in mind ! Enough ! But if you prate
    Praises of Florence, 'tis to wheedle me.
                A priceless jewel she :
Doubtless : but this you cannot understand :
For pigmy virtue grasps not aught so grand.

VII

A LUIGI DEL RICCIO

[1544]

Nel dolce d' una immensa cortesia,
    Dell' onor, della vita alcuna offesa
    S' asconde e cela spesso ; e tanto pesa,
    Che fa men cara la salute mia.
Chi gli omer' altru' 'mpenna, e po' tra via
    A lungo andar la rete occulta ha tesa ;
    L' ardente carità, d'amore accesa,
    Là più l' ammorza ov' arder più desia,
Però, Luigi mio, tenete chiara
    La prima grazia, ond' io la vita porto,
    Che non si turbi per tempesta o vento.
L' isdegnio ogni mercè vincere impara ;
    E, s' i' son ben del vero amico accorto,
    Mille piacer non vaglion un tormento.

VII

TO LUIGI DEL RICCIO

It happens that the sweet unfathomed sea
  Of seeming courtesy sometimes doth hide
  Offence to life and honour. This descried,
  I hold less dear the health restored to me.
He who lends wings of hope, while secretly
  He spreads a traitorous snare by the wayside,
  Hath dulled the flame of love, and mortified
  Friendship where friendship burns most fer-
      vently.
Keep then, my dear Luigi, clear and pure
  That ancient love to which my life I owe,
  That neither wind nor storm its calm may mar.
For wrath and pain our gratitude obscure ;
  And if the truest truth of love I know,
  One pang outweighs a thousand pleasures far.

VIII

IN MORTE DI CECCHINO BRACCI
A LUIGI DEL RICCIO
[1544]

A pena prima i begli occhi vidd' io,
 De' vostri aperti paradiso e vita,
 Che, chiusi el dì de l' ultima partita,
 Gli aperse in cielo a contemplare Iddio.
Conosco e piango ; e non fu l' error mio.
 Del cor sì tardi a lor beltà gradita ;
 Ma di morte anzi tempo, ond' è sparita
 A voi non già, m' al mie 'rdente desio.
Dunche, Luigi, a far l' unica forma
 Di Cecchin, di ch' i' parlo, in pietra viva
 Eterna, or ch' è già terra qui tra noi,
Se l'un nell' altro amato si trasforma,
 Po' che sanz' essa l' arte non v' arriva,
 Convien che per far lui retragga voi.

9

VIII

To Luigi del Riccio
AFTER THE DEATH OF CECCHINO BRACCI

Scarce had I seen for the first time his eyes
    Which to your living eyes were life and light,
    When closed at last in death's injurious night
    He opened them on God in Paradise.
I know it and I weep, too late made wise :
    Yet was the fault not mine ; for death's fell spite
    Robbed my desire of that supreme delight,
    Which in your better memory never dies.
Therefore, Luigi, if the task be mine
    To make unique Cecchino smile in stone
    For ever, now that earth hath made him dim,
If the beloved within the lover shine,
    Since art without him cannot work alone,
    You must I carve to tell the world of him.

IX

AL zucchero, alla mula, alle candele,
    Aggiuntovi un fiascon di malvagía,
    Resta sì vinta ogni fortuna mia,
    Ch' i' rendo le bilancie a san Michele.
Troppa bonaccia sgonfia sì le vele,
    Che senza vento in mar perde la via
    La debile mie barca, e par che sia
    Una festuca in mar rozza e crudele.
A rispetto alla grazia e al gran dono,
    Al cibo, al poto, e all' andar sovente,
    Ch' a ogni mio bisogno è caro e buono,
Signor mie car, ben vi sare' nïente
    Per merto a darvi tutto quel ch' io sono ;
    Chè 'l debito pagar, non è presente.

IX

THANKS FOR A GIFT

THE sugar, candles, and the saddled mule,
    Together with your cask of malvoisie,
    So far exceed all my necessity
    That Michael and not I my debt must rule.
In such a glassy calm the breezes fool
    My sinking sails, so that amid the sea
    My bark hath missed her way, and seems to be
    A wisp of straw whirled on a weltering pool.
To yield thee gift for gift and grace for grace,
    For food and drink and carriage to and fro,
    For all my need in every time and place,
O my dear lord, matched with the much I owe,
    All that I am were no real recompense :
    Paying a debt is not munificence.

X

A GANDOLFO PORRINO

RISPOSTA AL SONETTO PER LA MANCINA

La nuova alta beltà, che 'n ciel terrei
    Unica, non ch' al mondo iniquo e fello,
    (Suo nome dal sinistro braccio diello
    Il vulgo, cieco a non adorar lei)
Per voi sol veggio ; e far non la saprei
    Co' ferri in pietra, in carte col pennello ;
    Ma 'l vivo suo bel viso esser può quello,
    Nel qual vostro sperar fermar dovrei.
E se, come dal sole ogn' altra stella
    È vinta, vince l' intelletto nostro,
    Per voi non di men pregio esser dovea.
Dunque, a quietarvi, è suo beltà novella
    Da Dio formata a l' alto desir vostro ;
    E quel solo, e non io, far lo potea.

X

ON HIS MISTRESS FAUSTINA MANCINA

THAT new transcendent fair who seems to be
 Peerless in heaven as in this world of woe,
 (The common folk, too blind her worth to know
 And worship, called her Left Arm wantonly),
Was made, full well I know, for only thee :
 Nor could I carve or paint the glorious show
 Of that fair face : to life thou needs must go,
 To gain the favour thou dost crave of me.
If like the sun each star of heaven outshining,
 She conquers and outsoars our soaring thought,
 This bids thee rate her worth at its real price.
Therefore to satisfy thy ceaseless pining,
 Once more in heaven hath God her beauty
  wrought :
 God and not I can people Paradise.

XI

A GIORGIO VASARI

Per L'Opera Delle Vite de' Pittori,
Scultori ed Architettori
[1550]

Se con lo stile o coi colori avete
 Alla natura pareggiato l' arte,
 Anzi a quella scemato il pregio in parte
 Che 'l bel di lei più bello a noi rendete ;
Poi che con dota man posto vi sete
 A più degno lavoro, a vergar carte,
 Quel che vi manca, a lei di pregio in parte,
 Nel dar vita ad altrui, tutto togliete.
Che se secolo alcuno omai contese
 In far bell' opre, almen cedale, poi
 Che convien ch' al prescritto fine arrive.
Or le memorie altrui, già spente, accese
 Tornando, fate or che fien quelle, e voi,
 Malgrado d' essa, eternalmente vive.

12

XI

To Giorgio Vasari

ON THE LIVES OF THE PAINTERS

WITH pencil and with palette hitherto
  You made your art high Nature's paragon ;
  Nay more, from Nature her own prize you won,
  Making what she made fair more fair to view.
Now that your learnèd hand with labour new
  Of pen and ink a worthier work hath done,
  What erst you lacked, what still remained her
    own,
  The power of giving life, is gained for you.
If men in any age with Nature vied
  In beauteous workmanship, they had to yield
  When to the fated end years brought their name.
You, reilluming memories that died,
  In spite of Time and Nature have revealed
  For them and for yourself eternal fame.

12

XII

A Vittoria Colonna

Felice spirto, che con zelo ardente,
    Vecchio alla morte, in vita il mio cor tieni,
    E fra mill' altri tuo' diletti e beni
    Me sol saluti fra più nobil gente ;
Come mi fusti agli occhi, or alla mente,
    Per l' altru' fiate, a consolar mi vieni :
    Onde la speme il duol par che raffreni,
    Che non men che 'l disio l' anima sente.
Dunche trovando in te chi per me parla,
    Grazia di te per me fra tante cure,
    Tal grazia ne ringrazia chi ti scrive.
Che sconcia e grand' usur saria a farla,
    Donandoti turpissime pitture
    Per riaver persone belle e vive.

XII

A MATCHLESS COURTESY

Blest spirit, who with loving tenderness
    Quickenest my heart so old and near to die,
    Who mid thy joys on me dost bend an eye
    Though many nobler men around thee press !
As thou wert erewhile wont my sight to bless,
    So to console my mind thou now dost fly ;
    Hope therefore stills the pangs of memory,
    Which coupled with desire my soul distress.
So finding in thee grace to plead for me—
    Thy thoughts for me sunk in so sad a case—
    He who now writes, returns thee thanks for these.
Lo, it were foul and monstrous usury
    To send thee ugliest paintings in the place
    Of thy fair spirit's living phantasies.

XIII

ALLA MEDESIMA

PER esser manco almen, signiora, indegnio
  Dell' immensa vostr' alta cortesia,
    Prima, all' incontro a quella, usar la mia
    Con tutto il cor volse 'l mie basso ingegnio.
Ma visto poi c' ascendere a quel segnio
    Propio valor non è c' apra la via,
    Perdon domanda la mie colpa ria,
    E del fallir più saggio ognior divegnio.
E veggio ben com' erra, s' alcun crede
    La grazia, che da voi divina piove,
    Pareggi l' opra mia caduca e frale.
L' ingegnio e l' arte e la memoria cede :
    C' un don celeste mai con mille pruove
    Pagar può sol del suo chi è mortale.

XIII

To Vittoria Colonna

BRAZEN GIFTS FOR GOLDEN

SEEKING at least to be not all unfit
>For thy sublime and boundless courtesy,
>My lowly thoughts at first were fain to try
>What they could yield for grace so infinite.

But now I know my unassisted wit
>Is all too weak to make me soar so high ;
>For pardon, lady, for this fault I cry,
>And wiser still I grow remembering it.

Yea, well I see what folly 'twere to think
>That largess dropped from thee like dews from
>>heaven
>Could e'er be paid by work so frail as mine !

To nothingness my art and talent sink ;
>He fails who from his mortal stores hath given
>A thousandfold to match one gift divine.

XIV

ALLA MEDESIMA

[1550]

Da che concetto ha l' arte intera e diva
    La forma e gli atti d' alcun, poi di quello
    D' umil materia un semplice modello
    È 'l primo parto che da quel deriva.

Ma nel secondo poi di pietra viva
    S' adempion le promesse del martello ;
    E sì rinasce tal concetto e bello,
    Che ma' non è chi suo eterno prescriva.

Simil, di me model, nacqu' io da prima ;
    Di me model, per cosa più perfetta
    Da voi rinascer poi, donna alta e degna.

Se 'l poco accresce, e 'l mio superchio lima
    Vostra pietà ; qual penitenzia aspetta
    Mio fiero ardor, se mi gastiga e insegna ?

XIV

To VITTORIA COLONNA

THE MODEL AND THE STATUE

WHEN divine Art conceives a form and face,
 She bids the craftsman for his first essay
 To shape a simple model in mere clay :
 This is the earliest birth of Art's embrace.
From the live marble in the second place
 His mallet brings into the light of day
 A thing so beautiful that who can say
 When time shall conquer that immortal grace ?
Thus my own model I was born to be—
 The model of that nobler self, whereto
 Schooled by your pity, lady, I shall grow.
Each overplus and each deficiency
 You will make good.   What penance then is due
 For my fierce heat, chastened and taught by you ?

XIV

(SECONDA LEZIONE)

Se ben concetto ha la divina parte
    Il volto e gli atti d' alcun, po' di quello
    Doppio valor con breve e vil modello,
    Dà vita a' sassi, e non è forza d' arte.
Nè altrimenti in più rustiche carte,
    Anz' una pronta man prenda 'l pennello,
    Fra' dotti ingegni il più accorto e bello
    Prova e rivede, e sue storie comparte.
Simil di me model di poca stima
    Mie parto fu, per cosa alta e perfetta
    Da voi rinascer po', donna alta e degna.
Se 'l poco accresce, e 'l mio soperchio lima
    Vostra mercè ; qual penitenzia aspetta
    Mio fero ardor, se mi gastiga e 'nsegna ?

16

XIV

(SECOND READING)

To Vittoria Colonna

THE MODEL AND THE STATUE

When that which is divine in us doth try
    To shape a face, both brain and hand unite
    To give, from a mere model frail and slight,
    Life to the stone by Art's free energy.
Thus too before the painter dares to ply
    Paint-brush or canvas, he is wont to write
    Sketches on scraps of paper, and invite
    Wise minds to judge his figured history.
So, born a model rude and mean to be
    Of my poor self, I gain a nobler birth,
    Lady, from you, you fountain of all worth !
Each overplus and each deficiency
    You will make good.   What penance then is due
    For my fierce heat, chastened and taught by you ?

XV

Non ha l' ottimo artista alcun concetto,
    Ch' un marmo solo in sè non circonscriva
    Col suo soverchio ; e solo a quello arriva
    La man che ubbidisce all' intelletto.
Il mal ch' io fuggo, e 'l ben ch' io mi prometto,
    In te, donna leggiadra, altera e diva,
    Tal si nasconde ; e perch' io più non viva,
    Contraria ho l' arte al disiato effetto.
Amor dunque non ha, nè tua beltate,
    O durezza, o fortuna, o gran disdegno,
    Del mio mal colpa, o mio destino, o sorte ;
Se dentro del tuo cor morte e pietate
    Porti in un tempo, e che 'l mio basso ingegno
    Non sappia, ardendo, trarne altro che morte.

THE LOVER AND THE SCULPTOR

THE best of artists hath no thought to show
    Which the rough stone in its superfluous shell
    Doth not include : to break the marble spell
    Is all the hand that serves the brain can do.
The ill I shun, the good I seek, even so
    In thee, fair lady, proud, ineffable,
    Lies hidden : but the art I wield so well
    Works adverse to my wish, and lays me low.
Therefore not love, nor thy transcendent face,
    Nor cruelty, nor fortune, nor disdain,
    Cause my mischance, nor fate, nor destiny ;
Since in thy heart thou carriest death and grace
    Enclosed together, and my worthless brain
    Can draw forth only death to feed on me.

XVI

Sı come nella penna e nell' inchiostro
    È l' alto e 'l basso e 'l mediocre stile,
    E ne' marmi l' imagin ricca e vile,
    Secondo che 'l sa trar l' ingegnio nostro ;
Così, signior mie car, nel petto vostro,
    Quante l' orgoglio, è forse ogni atto umile :
    Ma io sol quel c' a me propio è e simile
    Ne traggo, come fuor nel viso mostro.
Chi semina sospir, lacrime e doglie,
    (L' umor dal ciel terreste, scietto e solo,
    A' vari semi vario si converte),
Però pianto e dolor ne miete e coglie :
    Chi mira alta beltà con sì gran duolo,
    Dubbie speranze, e pene acerbe e certe.

XVI

LOVE AND ART

As pen and ink alike serve him who sings
    In high or low or intermediate style ;
    As the same stone hath shapes both rich and vile
To match the fancies that each master brings ;
So, my loved lord, within thy bosom springs
    Pride mixed with meekness and kind thoughts
        that smile ;
    Whence I draw nought, my sad self to beguile,
But what my face shows—dark imaginings.
He who for seed sows sorrow, tears, and sighs,
    (The dews that fall from heaven, though pure
        and clear,
    From different germs take divers qualities)
Must needs reap grief and garner weeping eyes ;
    And he who looks on beauty with sad cheer,
    Gains doubtful hope and certain miseries.

XVII

Com' esser, donna, può quel ch' alcun vede
    Per lunga sperienza, che più dura
    L' immagin viva in pietra alpestra e dura,
    Che 'l suo fattor, che gli anni in cener riede ?
La causa all' effetto inclina e cede,
    Onde dall' arte è vinta la natura.
    Io 'l so, che 'l provo in la bella scultura ;
    Ch' all' opra il tempo e morte non tien fede.
Dunque posso ambo noi dar lunga vita
    In qual sie modo, o di colore o sasso,
    Di noi sembrando l' uno e l' altro volto :
Sì che mill' anni dopo la partita
    Quanto e voi bella fusti, e quant' io lasso
    Si veggia, e com' amarvi io non fui stolto.

XVII

THE ARTIST AND HIS WORK

How can that be, lady, which all men learn
    By long experience ?   Shapes that seem alive,
    Wrought in hard mountain marble, will survive
    Their maker, whom the years to dust return !
Thus to effect cause yields.   Art hath her turn,
    And triumphs over Nature.   I, who strive
    With Sculpture, know this well ; her wonders live
    In spite of time and death, those tyrants stern.
So I can give long life to both of us
    In either way, by colour or by stone,
    Making the semblance of thy face and mine.
Centuries hence when both are buried, thus
    Thy beauty and my sadness shall be shown,
    And men shall say, ' For her 'twas wise to pine.'

XVIII

Al cor di zolfo, alla carne di stoppa,
  All' ossa che di secco legno sieno,
  All' alma senza guida e senza freno,
  Al desir pronto, alla vaghezza troppa,
Alla cieca ragion debile e zoppa,
  Al visco, a' lacci di che 'l mondo è pieno,
  Non è gran maraviglia, in un baleno
  Arder nel primo foco che s' intoppa.
Alla bell' arte che, se dal ciel seco
  Ciascun la porta, vince la natura,
  Quantunque sè ben prema in ogni loco ;
S' io nacqui a quella nè sordo nè cieco,
  Proporzionato a chi 'l cor m' arde e fura,
  Colpa è di chi m' ha destinato al foco.

XVIII

BEAUTY AND THE ARTIST

A HEART of flaming sulphur, flesh of tow,
    Bones of dry wood, a soul without a guide
    To curb the fiery will, the ruffling pride
Of fierce desires that from the passions flow ;
A sightless mind that weak and lame doth go
    Mid snares and pitfalls scattered far and wide ;—
    What wonder if the first chance brand applied
To fuel massed like this should make it glow ?
Add beauteous art, which, brought with us from
        heaven,
    Will conquer nature ;—so divine a power
    Belongs to him who strives with every nerve.
If I was made for art, from childhood given
    A prey for burning beauty to devour,
    I blame the mistress I was born to serve.

XIX

Io mi son caro assai più ch' io non soglio ;
    Poi ch' io t' ebbi nel cor, più di me vaglio :
    Come pietra ch' aggiuntavi l' intaglio,
    È di più pregio che 'l suo primo scoglio.
O come scritta o pinta carta o foglio
    Più si riguarda d' ogni straccio o taglio ;
    Tal di me fo, da poi ch' io fui bersaglio
    Segnato dal tuo viso : e non mi doglio.
Sicur con tale stampa in ogni loco
    Vo come quel c' ha incanti o arme seco,
    Ch' ogni periglio gli fan venir meno.
I' vaglio contro all' acqua e contro al foco,
    Col segno tuo rallumino ogni cieco,
    E col mio sputo sano ogni veleno.

XIX

THE AMULET OF LOVE

FAR more than I was wont myself I prize :
    With you within my heart I rise in rate,
    Just as a gem engraved with delicate
    Devices o'er the uncut stone doth rise ;
Or as a painted sheet exceeds in price
    Each leaf left pure and in its virgin state :
    Such then am I since I was consecrate
    To be the mark for arrows from your eyes.
Stamped with your seal I'm safe where'er I go
    Like one who carries charms or coat of mail
    Against all dangers that his life assail.
Nor fire nor water now may work me woe ;
    Sight to the blind I can restore by you,
    Heal every wound, and every loss renew.

XX

Quanto si gode, lieta e ben contesta
    Di fior, sopra' crin d' or d' una, grillanda ;
    Che l' altro inanzi l' uno all' altro manda,
    Come ch' il primo sia a baciar la testa !
Contenta è tutto il giorno quella vesta
    Che serra 'l petto, e poi par che si spanda ;
    E que c' oro filato si domanda
    Le guanci' e 'l collo di toccar non resta.
Ma più lieto quel nastro par che goda,
    Dorato in punta, con sì fatte tempre,
    Che preme e tocca il petto ch' egli allaccia.
E la schietta cintura che s' annoda.
    Mi par dir seco : qui vo' stringier sempre !
    Or che farebbon dunche le mie braccia ?

XX

THE GARLAND AND THE GIRDLE

What joy hath yon glad wreath of flowers that is
    Around her golden hair so deftly twined,
    Each blossom pressing forward from behind,
    As though to be the first her brows to kiss !
The livelong day her dress hath perfect bliss,
    That now reveals her breast, now seems to bind :
    And that fair woven net of gold refined
    Rests on her cheek and throat in happiness !
Yet still more blissful seems to me the band
    Gilt at the tips, so sweetly doth it ring
    And clasp the bosom that it serves to lace :
Yea, and the belt to such as understand,
    Bound round her waist, saith : here I'd ever
        cling.—
    What would my arms do in that girdle's place ?

XXI

D' ALTRUI pietoso e sol di sè spietato
    Nascie un vil bruto, che con dolce doglia
    L' altrui man veste, e la suo scorza spoglia,
    E sol per morte si può dir ben nato.
Così volesse al mie signior mie fato
    Vestir suo viva di mie morta spoglia ;
    Che, come serpe al sasso si discoglia,
    Pur per morte potria cangiar mie stato.
O fussi sol la mie l' irsuta pelle
    Che, del suo pel contesta, fa tal gonna
    Che con ventura stringe sì bel seno,
Che 'l giorno pur m' aresti ; o le pianelle
    Fuss' io, che basa a quel fanno e colonna,
    C' al piover t' are' pur addosso almeno !

XXI

THE SILKWORM

KIND to the world, but to itself unkind,
 A worm is born, that dying noiselessly
 Despoils itself to clothe fair limbs, and be
In its true worth by death alone divined.
Oh, would that I might die, for her to find
 Raiment in my outworn mortality !
 That, changing like the snake, I might be free
To cast the slough wherein I dwell confined !
Nay, were it mine, that shaggy fleece that stays,
 Woven and wrought into a vestment fair,
 Around her beauteous bosom in such bliss !
All through the day she'd clasp me ! Would I were
 The shoes that bear her burden ! When the ways
 Were wet with rain, her feet I then should kiss !

XXII

Se nel volto per gli occhi il cor si vede,
   Altro segnio non ho più manifesto
   Della mie fiamma : addunche basti or questo,
   Signior mie caro, a domandar mercede.
Forse lo spirto tuo, con maggior fede
   Ch' i' non credo, che sguarda il foco onesto
   Che m' arde, fie di me pietoso e presto ;
   Come grazia ch' abbonda a chi ben chiede.
O felice quel dì, se questo è certo !
   Fermisi in un momento il tempo e l' ore,
   Il giorno e 'l sol nella su' antica traccia ;
Accio ch' i' abbi, e non già per mie merto,
   Il desiato mie dolce signiore
   Per sempre nell' indegnie e pronte braccia.

XXII

WAITING IN FAITH

IF through the eyes the heart speaks clear and true,
    I have no stronger sureties than these eyes
    For my pure love.   Prithee let them suffice,
Lord of my soul, pity to gain from you.
More tenderly perchance than is my due,
    Your spirit sees into my heart, where rise
    The flames of holy worship, nor denies
The grace reserved for those who humbly sue.
Oh, blessèd day when you at last are mine !
    Let time stand still, and let noon's chariot stay ;
    Fixed be that moment on the dial of heaven !
That I may clasp and keep, by grace divine,
    Clasp in these yearning arms and keep for aye
    My heart's loved lord to me desertless given !

XXIII

BEN posson gli occhi mia presso e lontano
   Veder dove apparisce il tuo bel volto ;
   Ma dove lor, a' piè, donna, è ben tolto
   Portar le braccia e l' una e l' altra mano.
L' anima, l' intelletto intero e sano
   Per gli occhi ascende più libero e sciolto
   All' alta tuo beltà ; ma l' ardor molto
   Non dà tal privilegio al corpo umano
Grave e mortal ; sì che mal segue poi
   Senz' ale ancor d' un' angioletta il volo,
   E 'l veder sol pur se ne gloria e loda.
Deh ! se tu puoi nel ciel quanto tra noi,
   Fa' del mio corpo tutto un occhio solo ;
   Nè fia poi parte in me che non ti goda.

XXIII

FLESH AND SPIRIT

WELL may these eyes of mine both near and far
    Behold the beams that from thy beauty flow ;
    But, lady, feet must halt where sight may go :
    We see, but cannot climb to clasp a star.
The pure ethereal soul surmounts that bar
    Of flesh, and soars to where thy splendours glow,
    Free through the eyes ; while prisoned here
       below,
    Though fired with fervent love, our bodies are.
Clogged with mortality and wingless, we
    Cannot pursue an angel in her flight :
    Only to gaze exhausts our utmost might.
Yet, if but heaven like earth incline to thee,
    Let my whole body be one eye to see,
    That not one part of me may miss thy sight !

XXIV

Spirto ben nato, in cui si specchia e vede
    Nelle tuo belle membre oneste e care
    Quante natura e 'l ciel tra no' può fare,
    Quand' a null' altra suo bell' opra cede :
Spirto leggiadro, in cui si spera e crede
    Dentro, come di fuor nel viso appare,
    Amor, pietà, mercè ; cose sì rare,
    Che ma' furn' in beltà con tanta fede :
L' amor mi prende, e la beltà mi lega ;
    La pietà, la mercè con dolci sguardi
    Ferma speranz' al cor par che ne doni.
Qual uso o qual governo al mondo niega,
    Qual crudeltà per tempo, o qual più tardi,
    C' a sì bel viso morte non perdoni ?

XXIV

THE DOOM OF BEAUTY

CHOICE soul, in whom, as in a glass, we see,
    Mirrored in thy pure form and delicate,
    What beauties heaven and nature can create,
    The paragon of all their works to be !
Fair soul, in whom love, pity, piety,
    Have found a home, as from thy outward state
    We clearly read, and are so rare and great
    That they adorn none other like to thee !
Love takes me captive ; beauty binds my soul ;
    Pity and mercy with their gentle eyes
    Wake in my heart a hope that cannot cheat.
What law, what destiny, what fell control,
    What cruelty, or late or soon, denies
    That death should spare perfection so complete ?

XXV

Dimmi di grazia, amor, se gli occhi mei
    Veggono 'l ver della beltà ch' aspiro,
    O s' io l' ho dentro allor che, dov' io miro,
    Veggio più bello el viso di costei.
Tu 'l de' saper, po' che tu vien con lei
    A torm' ogni mie pace, ond' io m' adiro ;
    Nè vorre' manco un minimo sospiro,
    Nè men ardente foco chiederei.
La beltà che tu vedi è ben da quella ;
    Ma crescie poi ch' a miglior loco sale,
    Se per gli occhi mortali all' alma corre.
Quivi si fa divina, onesta e bella,
    Com' a sè simil vuol cosa immortale :
    Questa, e non quella, a gli occhi tuo' precorre.

XXV

THE TRANSFIGURATION OF BEAUTY

A DIALOGUE WITH LOVE

NAY, prithee tell me, Love, when I behold
    My lady, do mine eyes her beauty see
    In truth, or dwells that loveliness in me
Which multiplies her grace a thousandfold ?
Thou needs must know ; for thou with her of old
    Comest to stir my soul's tranquillity ;
    Yet would I not seek one sigh less, or be
By loss of that loved flame more simply cold.—
The beauty thou decernest, all is hers ;
    But grows in radiance as it soars on high
    Through mortal eyes unto the soul above :
'Tis there transfigured ; for the soul confers
    On what she holds, her own divinity :
    And this transfigured beauty wins thy love.

XXVI

Non men grazia, donna, che gran doglia
  Ancide alcun, che 'l furto a morte mena,
  Privo di speme e ghiacciato ogni vena,
  Se vien subito scampo che 'l discioglia.
Simil se tua mercè, più che ma' soglia,
  Nella miseria mie d' affanni piena
  Con soverchia pietà mi rasserena,
  Par, più che 'l pianger, la vita mi toglia.
Così n' avvien di novell' aspra e dolce ;
  Ne' lor contrari è morte in un momento,
  Onde s' allarga o troppo stringe il core.
Tal tua beltà, ch' amore e 'l ciel qui folce,
  Se mi vuol vivo, affreni il gran contento ;
  Ch' al don superchio debil virtù muore.

XXVI

JOY MAY KILL

Too much good luck no less than misery
    May kill a man condemned to mortal pain,
    If, lost to hope and chilled in every vein,
    A sudden pardon comes to set him free.
Thus thy unwonted kindness shown to me
    Amid the gloom where only sad thoughts reign,
    With too much rapture bringing light again,
    Threatens my life more than that agony.
Good news and bad may bear the self-same knife ;
    And death may follow both upon their flight ;
    For hearts that shrink or swell, alike will break.
Let then thy beauty, to preserve my life,
    Temper the source of this supreme delight,
    Lest joy so poignant slay a soul so weak.

XXVII

Non posso altra figura immaginarmi,
    O di nud' ombra o di terrestre spoglia,
    Col più alto pensier, tal che mie voglia
    Contra la tuo beltà di quella s' armi.
Che, da te mosso, tanto sciender parmi,
    Ch' amor d' ogni valor mi priva e spoglia
    Ond' a pensar di minuir mie doglia,
    Duplicando, la morte viene a darmi.
Però non val che più sproni mie fuga,
    Doppiando 'l corso alla beltà nemica;
    Chè 'l men dal più velocie non si scosta.
Amor con le sue man gli occhi m' asciuga,
    Promettendomi cara ogni fatica;
    Chè vile esser non può chi tanto costa.

XXVII

NO ESCAPE FROM LOVE

I CANNOT by the utmost flight of thought
    Conceive another form of air or clay,
    Wherewith against thy beauty to array
    My wounded heart in armour fancy-wrought :
For, lacking thee, so low my state is brought,
    That Love hath stolen all my strength away ;
    Whence, when I fain would halve my griefs, they weigh
    With double sorrow, and I sink to nought.
Thus all in vain my soul to scape thee flies,
    For ever faster flies her beauteous foe :
    From the swift-footed feebly run the slow !
Yet with his hands Love wipes my weeping eyes,
    Saying, this toil will end in happy cheer ;
    What costs the heart so much must needs be dear !

XXVIII

La vita del mie amor non è 'l cor mio,
>Ch' amor, di quel ch' io t' amo, è senza core ;
>Dov' è cosa mortal piena d' errore,
>Esser non può già ma', nè pensier rio.
Amor nel dipartir l' alma di Dio
>Me fe' san occhio, e te luc' e splendore ;
>Nè può non rivederlo in quel che muore
>Di te, per nostro mal, mie gran disio.
Come dal foco el caldo esser diviso
>Non può, dal bell' etterno ogni mie stima,
>Ch' esalta, ond 'ella vien, chi più 'l somiglia.
Tu c' hai negli occhi tutto 'l paradiso,
>Per ritornar là dov' i' t' ama' prima,
>Ricorro ardendo sott' alle tuo ciglia.

XXVIII

THE HEAVENLY BIRTH OF LOVE
AND BEAUTY

THIS heart of flesh feeds not with life my love :
    The love wherewith I love thee hath no heart ;
    Nor harbours it in any mortal part,
    Where erring thought or ill desire may move.
When first Love sent our souls from God above,
    He fashioned me to see thee as thou art—
    Pure light ; and thus I find God's counterpart
    In thy fair face, and feel the sting thereof.
As heat from fire, from loveliness divine
    The mind that worships what recalls the sun
    From whence she sprang, can be divided never :
And since thine eyes all Paradise enshrine,
    Burning unto those orbs of light I run,
    There where I loved thee first to dwell for ever.

XXIX

I' MI credetti, il primo giorno ch' io
    Mira' tante bellezze uniche e sole,
    Fermar gli occhi, com' aquila nel sole,
    Nella minor di tante ch' i' desio.
Po' conosciut' ho il fallo e l'erro mio ;
    Chè chi senz' ale un angel seguir vole,
    Il seme a' sassi, al vento le parole
    Indarno ispargie, e l' intelletto a Dio.
Dunche, s' appresso il cor non mi sopporta
    L' infinita beltà, che gli occhi abbaglia,
    Nè di lontan par m' assicuri o fidi ;
Che fie di me ? qual guida o quale scorta
    Fie che con teco ma' mi giovi o vaglia,
    S' appresso m' ardi, e nel partir m' uccidi ?

XXIX

LOVE'S DILEMMA

I DEEMED upon that day when first I knew
  So many peerless beauties blent in one
  That, like an eagle gazing on the sun,
  Mine eyes might fix on the least part of you.
That dream hath vanished, and my hope is flown ;
  For he who fain a seraph would pursue
  Wingless, hath cast words to the winds, and dew
  On stones, and gauged God's reason with his own.
If then my heart cannot endure the blaze
  Of beauties infinite that blind these eyes,
  Nor yet can bear to be from you divided,
What fate is mine ?   Who guides or guards my ways,
  Seeing my soul, so lost and ill-betided,
  Burns in your presence, in your absence dies ?

XXX

Veggio co' bei vostri occhi un dolce lume,
 Che co' miei ciechi già veder non posso ;
 Porto co' vostri piedi un pondo a dosso,
 Che de' mie' zoppi non è già costume ;
Volo con le vostr' ale senza piume ;
 Col vostr' ingegno al ciel sempre son mosso ;
 Dal vostr' arbitrio son pallido e rosso ;
 Freddo al sol, caldo alle più fredde brume.
Nel voler vostro è sol la voglia mia,
 I mie' pensier nel vostro cor si fanno,
 Nel vostro fiato son le mia parole.
Come luna da sè sol par ch' io sia ;
 Chè gli occhi nostri in ciel veder non sanno
 Se non quel tanto che n' accende il sole.

XXX

LOVE THE LIGHT-GIVER

With your fair eyes a charming light I see,
 For which my own blind eyes would peer in vain ;
 Stayed by your feet the burden I sustain
 Which my lame feet find all too strong for me ;
Wingless upon your pinions forth I fly ;
 Heavenward your spirit stirreth me to strain ;
 E'en as you will I blush and blanch again,
 Freeze in the sun, burn 'neath a frosty sky.
Your will includes and is the lord of mine ;
 Life to my thoughts within your heart is given ;
 My words begin to breathe upon your breath :
Like to the moon am I, that cannot shine
 Alone ; for lo ! our eyes see nought in heaven
 Save what the living sun illumineth.

XXXI

A che più debb' io mai l' intensa voglia
  Sfogar con pianti o con parole meste,
  Se di tal sorte 'l ciel, che l' alma veste,
  Tard' o per tempo, alcun mai non ne spoglia ?
A che 'l cor lass' a più morir m' invoglia,
  S' altri pur dee morir ? Dunque per queste
  Luci l' ore del fin fian men moleste ;
  Ch' ogn' altro ben val men ch' ogni mia doglia.
Però se 'l colpo, ch' io ne rub' e 'nvolo,
  Schifar non poss' ; almen, s' è destinato,
  Chi entreran fra la dolcezza e 'l duolo ?
Se vint' e pres' i' debb' esser beato,
  Maraviglia non è se', nud' e solo,
  Resto prigion d' un Cavalier armato.

XXXI

LOVE'S LORDSHIP

Why should I seek to ease intense desire
    With still more tears and windy words of grief,
    When heaven, or late or soon, sends no relief
    To souls whom love hath robed around with fire ?
Why need my aching heart to death aspire,
    When all must die ?   Nay, death beyond belief
    Unto these eyes would be both sweet and brief,
    Since in my sum of woes all joys expire !
Therefore because I cannot shun the blow
    I rather seek, say who must rule my breast,
    Gliding between her gladness and her woe ?
If only chains and bands can make me blest,
    No marvel if alone and bare I go
    An armèd Knight's captive and slave confessed.

XXXII

S' UN casto amor, s' una pietà superna,
 S' una fortuna infra dua amanti equale,
 S' un' aspra sorte all' un dell' altro cale,
 S' un spirto, s' un voler duo cor governa ;
S' un' anima in duo corpi è fatta eterna,
 Ambo levando al cielo e con pari ale :
 S' amor d' un colpo e d' un dorato strale
 Le viscier di duo petti arda e discierna ;
S' amar l' un l' altro, e nessun se medesmo,
 D' un gusto e d' un diletto, a tal mercede,
 C' a un fin voglia l' uno e l' altro porre ;
Se mille e mille non sarien centesmo
 A tal nodo d' amore, a tanta fede ;
 E sol l' isdegnio il può rompere e sciorre ?

XXXII

LOVE'S EXPOSTULATION

If love be chaste, if virtue conquer ill,
 If fortune bind both lovers in one bond,
 If either at the other's grief despond,
 If both be governed by one life, one will ;
If in two bodies one soul triumph still,
 Raising the twain from earth to heaven beyond,
 If Love with one blow and one golden wand
 Have power both smitten breasts to pierce and
  thrill ;
If each the other love, himself forgoing,
 With such delight, such savour, and so well,
 That both to one sole end their wills combine ;
If thousands of these thoughts, all thought outgoing,
 Fail the least part of their firm love to tell :
 Say, can mere angry spite this knot untwine ?

XXXIII

(PRIMA LEZIONE)

PERCHÈ tuo gran bellezze al mondo sieno
    In donna più cortese e manco dura,
    Prego se ne ripigli la natura
    Tutte quelle ch' ogn' or ti vengon meno ;
E serbi a riformar del tuo sereno
    E divin volto una gientil figura
    Del ciel, e sia d' amor perpetua cura
    Rifarne un cor di grazia e pietà pieno.
E serbi poi i miei sospiri ancora,
    E le lacrime sparte insieme accoglia,
    E doni a chi quella ami un' altra volta.
Forse a pietà chi nascierà 'n quell' ora
    La moverà con la mie propria doglia ;
    Nè fia persa la grazia ch' or m' è tolta.

XXXIII

(FIRST READING)

A PRAYER TO NATURE

AMOR REDIVIVUS

THAT thy great beauty on our earth may be
    Shrined in a lady softer and more kind,
    I call on nature to collect and bind
    All those delights the slow years steal from thee,
And save them to restore the radiancy
    Of thy bright face in some fair form designed
    By heaven ; and may Love ever bear in mind
    To mould her heart of grace and courtesy.
I call on nature too to keep my sighs,
    My scattered tears to take and recombine,
    And give to him who loves that fair again :
More happy he perchance shall move those eyes
    To mercy by the griefs wherewith I pine,
    Nor lose the kindness that from me is ta'en !

XXXIII

SOL perchè tue bellezze al mondo sieno
    Eterne al tempo che la dona e fura,
    Credo che se ne ripigli la natura
    Tutto quel ch' ogni giorno a te vien meno ;
E serbi al parto d' un più largo seno
    Con miglior sorte, e con più strema cura,
    Per riformar di nuovo una figura
    Ch' abbi 'l tuo volto angelico e sereno.
Deh ! serbi 'l cielo i miei sospiri ancora,
    E le lacrime sparte mie raccoglia,
    E doni a chi queste ami un' altra volta.
Forse a pietà chi nascerà 'n quell' ora
    La moverà con la mia strema doglia,
    Nè fie persa la grazia ch' or m' è tolta !

XXXIII

(SECOND READING)

A PRAYER TO NATURE

AMOR REDIVIVUS

IF only that thy beauties here may be
    Deathless through Time that rends the wreaths
        he twined,
    I trust that Nature will collect and bind
    All those delights the slow years steal from
        thee,
And keep them for a birth more happily
    Born under better auspices, refined
    Into a heavenly form of nobler mind,
    And dowered with all thine angel purity.
Ah me ! and may heaven also keep my sighs,
    My scattered tears preserve and reunite,
    And give to him who loves that fair again !
More happy he perchance shall move those eyes
    To mercy by the griefs my manhood blight,
    Nor lose the kindness that from me is ta'en !

XXXIV

Sì amico al freddo sasso è 'l foco interno,
 Che di quel tratto, se lo circunscrive,
 Che l' arda e spezzi, in qualche modo vive,
 Legando con sè gli altri, in loco eterno.
E se 'n fornace dura, istate e verno
 Vince, e 'n più pregio che prima s' ascrive ;
 Come purgata, infra l' altre alte e dive
 Alma nel ciel tornasse da l' inferno.
Così tratto da me, se mi disolve
 Il foco che m' è dentro occulto gioco,
 Arso e po' spento aver più vita posso.
Dunche, s' i' vivo fatto fummo e polve,
 Eterno ben sarò, s' induro al foco ;
 Da tale oro e non ferro son percosso.

XXXIV

LOVE'S FURNACE

So friendly is the fire to flinty stone,
    That, struck therefrom and kindled to a blaze,
    It burns the stone, and from the ash doth raise
    What lives thenceforward binding stones in one :
Kiln-hardened this resists both frost and sun,
    Acquiring higher worth for endless days—
    As the purged soul from hell returns with praise,
    Amid the heavenly host to take her throne.
E'en so the fire struck from my soul, that lay
    Close-hidden in my heart, may temper me,
    Till burned and slaked to better life I rise.
If, made mere smoke and dust, I live to-day,
    Fire-hardened I shall live eternally ;
    Such gold not iron, my spirit strikes and tries.

XXXV

SENTO d' un foco un freddo aspetto acceso
　　Che lontan m' arde, e sè con seco agghiaccia ;
　　Provo una forza in dua leggiadre braccia,
　　Che muove senza moto ogni altro peso :
Unico spirto, e da me solo inteso
　　Che non ha morte, e morte altrui procaccia,
　　Veggio ; e truovo chi, sciolto, il cor m' allaccia ;
　　E da chi giova sol mi sento offeso.
Com' esser può, signor, che d'un bel volto
　　Ne port' il mio così contrari effetti,
　　Se mal può chi non gli ha donarli altrui ?
Onde al mio viver lieto, che m' ha tolto,
　　Fa forse come 'l sol, se nol permetti,
　　Che scalda 'l mondo, e non è caldo lui.

XXXV

LOVE'S PARADOXES

Far off with fire I feel a cold face lit,
>   That makes me burn, the while itself doth
>   freeze :
>   Two fragile arms enchain me, which with ease,
>   Unmoved themselves, can move weights infinite
A soul none knows but I, most exquisite,
>   That, deathless, deals me death, my spirit sees :
>   I meet with one who, free, my heart doth seize :
>   And who alone can cheer, hath tortured it.
How can it be that from one face like thine
>   My own should feel effects so contrary,
>   Since ill comes not from things devoid of ill ?
That loveliness perchance doth make me pine,
>   Even as the sun, whose fiery beams we see,
>   Inflames the world, while he is temperate still.

XXXVI

Se l' immortal desio, c' alza e correggie
    Gli altrui pensier, traessi e mie' di fore,
    Forse c' ancor nella casa d' amore
    Faria pietoso chi spietato reggie.
Ma perchè l' alma per divina leggie
    Ha lunga vita, e 'l corpo in breve muore,
    Non può 'l senso suo lode o suo valore
    Appien descriver, quel c' appien non leggie.
Dunque, ohimè! come sarà udita
    La casta voglia che 'l cor dentro incende
    Da chi sempre se stesso in altrui vede?
La mia cara giornata m' è 'mpedita
    Col mio signor, ch' alle menzogne attende;
    Ch' a dire il ver, bugiardo è chi nol crede.

XXXVI

LOVE MISINTERPRETED

IF the undying thirst that purifies
>   Our mortal thoughts, could draw mine to the
>   day,
>   Perchance the lord who now holds cruel sway
>   In Love's high house, would prove more kindly-
>   wise.

But since the laws of heaven immortalise
>   Our souls, and doom our flesh to swift decay,
>   Tongue cannot tell how fair, how pure as day,
>   Is the soul's thirst that far beyond it lies.

How then, ah wo is me ! shall that chaste fire,
>   Which burns the heart within me, be made
>   known,
>   If sense finds only sense in what it sees ?

All my fair hours are turned to miseries
>   With my loved lord, who minds but lies alone ;
>   For, truth to tell, who trusts not is a liar.

XXXVII

S' ALCUN legato è pur dal piacer molto,
  Come da morte altrui tornare in vita ;
  Qual cosa è, che poi paghi tanta aita,
  Che renda il debitor libero e sciolto ?
E se pur fusse, ne sarebbe tolto
  Il soprastar d' una mercè infinita
  Al ben servito ; onde sarie impedita
  Dall' incontro servire a quella volto.
Dunque, per tener alta vostra grazia,
  Donna, sopra l' mio stato, in me sol bramo
  Ingratitudin più che cortesia.
Chè dove l' un dell' altro al par si sazia,
  Non mi sare' signor quel che tanto amo :
  Chè in parità non cape signoria.

XXXVII

PERHAPS TO VITTORIA COLONNA

LOVE'S SERVITUDE

HE who is bound by some great benefit,
    As to be raised from death to life again,
    How shall he recompense that gift, or gain
    Freedom from servitude so infinite ?
Yet if 'twere possible to pay the debt,
    He'd lose that kindness which we entertain
    For those who serve us well : since it is plain
    That kindness needs some boon to quicken it.
Wherefore, O lady, to maintain thy grace,
    So far above my fortune, what I bring
    Is rather thanklessness than courtesy :
For if both met as equals face to face,
    She whom I love could not be called my king ;—
    There is no lordship in equality.

XXXVIII

RENDETE a gli occhi miei, o fonte o fiume,
    L' onde della non vostra e salda vena,
    Che più v' innalza, e cresce, e con più lena
    Che non è 'l vostro natural costume.
E tu, folt' air, che 'l celeste lume
    Tempri a' tristi occhi, de' sospir miei piena,
    Rendigli al cor mio lasso, e rasserena
    Tua scura faccia al mio visivo acume.
Renda la terra i passi a le mie piante,
    Ch' ancor l' erba germogli che gli è tolta ;
    E' l suono Ecco, già sorda a' miei lamenti ;
Gli sguardi a gli occhi mie', tue luci sante ;
    Ch' io possa altra bellezza un' altra volta
    Amar, po' che di me non ti contenti.

XXXVIII

LOVE'S VAIN EXPENSE

Give back unto mine eyes, ye fount and rill,
Those streams, not yours, that are so full and
strong,
That swell your springs, and roll your waves along
With force unwonted in your native hill !
And thou, dense air, weighed with my sighs so chill,
That hidest heaven's own light thick mists
among,
Give back those sighs to my sad heart, nor wrong
My visual ray with thy dark face of ill !
Let earth give back the footprints that I wore,
That the bare grass I spoiled may sprout again ;
And Echo, now grown deaf, my cries return !
Loved eyes, unto mine eyes those looks restore,
And let me woo another not in vain,
Since how to please thee I shall never learn !

XXXIX

La ragion meco si lamenta e dole,
    Parte ch' i' spero amando esser felice ;
    Con forti esempli e con vere parole
    La mie vergognia mi ramenta, e dice :
Che ne riportera' dal vivo sole,
    Altro che morte ? e non come fenice.
    Ma poco giova : chè chi cader vuole,
    Non basta l' altrui man pront' e vitrice.
I' conosco e mie' danni, e 'l vero intendo :
    Dall' altra banda, albergo un altro core,
    Che più m' uccide dove più m' arrendo.
In mezzo di duo mort' è 'l mie signiore ;
    Questa non voglio, e questa non comprendo :
    Così sospeso, il corpo e l' alma muore.

XXXIX

LOVE'S ARGUMENT WITH REASON

Reason laments and grieves full sore with me,
    The while I hope by loving to be blest ;
    With precepts sound and true philosophy
    My shame she quickens thus within my breast :
' What else but death will that sun deal to thee—
    Nor like the phœnix in her flaming nest ? '
    Yet nought avails this wise morality ;
    No hand can save a suicide confessed.
I know my doom ; the truth I apprehend :
    But on the other side my traitorous heart
    Slays me whene'er to wisdom's words I bend.
Between two deaths my lady stands apart :
    This death I dread ; that none can comprehend.
    In this suspense body and soul must part.

XL

Non so se s' è la desiata luce
    Del suo primo fattor, che l' alma sente ;
    O se dalla memoria della gente
    Alcun' altra beltà nel cor traluce ;
O se fama o se sognio alcun prodduce
    Agli occhi manifesto, al cor presente ;
    Di sè lasciando un non so che cocente,
    Ch' è forse or quel ch' a pianger mi conduce ;
Quel ch' i' sento e ch' i' cerco : e chi mi guidi
    Meco non è ; nè so ben veder dove
    Trovar mel possa, e par c' altri mel mostri.
Questo, signior, m' avvien, po' ch' i' vi vidi ;
    C' un dolce amaro, un sì e no mi muove :
    Certo saranno stati gli occhi vostri.

XL

(FIRST READING)

LOVE'S LOADSTONE

I KNOW not if it be the longed-for light
  Of her first Maker which the spirit feels ;
  Or if a time-old memory reveals
  Some other beauty for the heart's delight ;
Or fame or dreams beget that vision bright,
  Sweet to the eyes, which through the bosom
      steals,
  Leaving I know not what that wounds and heals,
  And now perchance hath made me weep outright.
Be this what this may be, 'tis this I seek :
  Nor guide have I ; nor know I where to find
  That burning fire ; yet some one seems to lead.
This, since I saw thee, lady, makes me weak ;
  A bitter-sweet sways here and there my mind,
  And sure I am thine eyes this mischief breed.

XL

(SECONDA LEZIONE)

NON so se s' è l' immaginata luce,
 Che più e meno ogni persona sente ;
 O se dalla memoria o dalla mente
 Alcun' altra beltà nel cor traluce ;
O se nell' alma ancor risplende e luce
 Del suo prestino stato il foco ardente,
 C' a sì caldo desir tiri sovente
 Ogni ottimo pensier, c' al ver conduce ;
Ch' i' brami e cerchi, e non so chi mi guidi :
 Il foco che pur m' arde, è non so dove ;
 Nè so 'l cammino, e par c' altri mel mostri.
Questo, donna, m' avvien po' ch' i' vi vidi ;
 C' un dolcie amaro, un sì e no mi muove :
 Certo saranno stati gli occhi vostri.

XL

(SECOND READING)

LOVE'S LOADSTONE

I KNOW not if it be the fancied light
 Which every man or more or less doth feel ;
 Or if the mind and memory reveal
 Some other beauty for the heart's delight ;
Or if within the soul the vision bright
 Of her celestial home once more doth steal,
 Drawing our better thoughts with pure appeal
 To the true Good above all mortal sight :
This light I long for and unguided seek ;
 This fire that burns my heart, I cannot find ;
 Nor know the way, though some one seems to
   lead.
This, since I saw thee, lady, makes me weak :
 A bitter-sweet sways here and there my mind ;
 And sure I am thine eyes this mischief breed.

XLI

Colui che fece, e non di cosa alcuna,
  Il tempo che non era anzi a nessuno,
  Ne fe d' un due : e diè 'l sol alto all' uno ;
  All' altro, assai più presso, diè la luna.
Onde 'l caso, la sorte e la fortuna
  In un momento nacquer di ciascuno ;
  Et a me consegnaro il tempo bruno,
  Come a simil nel parto e nella cuna.
E come quel che contrafà se stesso,
  Quando è ben notte più buio esser suole ;
  Ond' io di far ben mal m' affligo e lagno.
Pur mi consola assai l' esser concesso
  Far giorno chiar mia oscura notte al sole
  Ch' a voi fu dato al nascer per compagno.

XLI

LIGHT AND DARKNESS

He who ordained, when first the world began,
    Time, that was not before creation's hour,
    Divided it, and gave the sun's high power
    To rule the one, the moon the other span :
Thence fate and changeful chance and fortune's ban
    Did in one moment down on mortals shower :
    To me they portioned darkness for a dower ;
    Dark hath my lot been since I was a man.
Myself am ever mine own counterfeit ;
    And as deep night grows still more dim and dun,
    So still of more misdoing must I rue :
Meanwhile this solace to my soul is sweet,
    That my black night doth make more clear the
        sun
    Which at your birth was given to wait on you.

XLII

Ogni van chiuso, ogni coperto loco,
    Quantunque ogni materia circunscrive,
    Serba la notte quando il giorno vive,
    Contro al solar suo luminoso gioco.
E s' ella è vinta pur da fiamma o foco,
    Da lei, dal sol son discacciate e prive
    Con più vil cosa ancor, sue specie dive,
    Tal ch' ogni verme assai ne rompe o poco.
Quel che resta scoperto al sol, che ferve
    Per mille varii semi e mille piante,
    Il fier bifolco con l' aratro assale ;
Ma l' ombra sol a piantar l' uomo serve.
    Dunque le notti più ch' e dì son sante,
    Quanto l' uom più d' ogni altro frutto vale.

XLII

SACRED NIGHT

ALL hollow vaults and dungeons sealed from sight,
    All caverns circumscribed with roof and wall,
    Defend dark Night, though noon around her fall,
    From the fierce play of solar day-beams bright.
But if she be assailed by fire or light,
    Her powers divine are nought ; they tremble all
    Before things far more vile and trivial—
    Even a glow-worm can confound their might.
The earth that lies bare to the sun, and breeds
    A thousand germs that burgeon and decay—
    This earth is wounded by the ploughman's share :
But only darkness serves for human seeds ;
    Night therefore is more sacred far than day,
    Since man excels all fruits however fair.

XLIII

Perchè Febo non torc' e non distende
 D' intorn' a questo globo fredd' e molle
 Le braccia sua lucenti, el vulgo volle
 Notte chiamar quel sol che non comprende.
E tant' è debol, che s' alcun accende
 Un picciol torchio, in quella parte tolle
 La vita dalla nott' ; e tant' è folle,
 Che l' esca col fucil la squarcia e fende.
E se gli è pur che qualche cosa sia,
 Cert' è figlia del sol e della terra ;
 Chè l' un tien l' ombra, e l' altro sol la cria
Ma sia che vuol, che pur chi la loda erra ;
 Vedova, scur', in tanta gelosia,
 Ch' una lucciola sol gli può far guerra.

XLIII

THE IMPEACHMENT OF NIGHT

WHAT time bright Phœbus doth not stretch and bend
  His shining arms around this terrene sphere,
  The people call that season dark and drear
  Night, for the cause they do not comprehend.
So weak is Night that if our hand extend
  A glimmering torch, her shadows disappear,
  Leaving her dead ; like frailest gossamere,
  Tinder and steel her mantle rive and rend.
Nay, if this Night be anything at all,
  Sure she is daughter of the sun and earth ;
  This holds, the other spreads that shadowy pall.
Howbeit they err who praise this gloomy birth,
  So frail and desolate and void of mirth
  That one poor firefly can her might appal.

XLIV

O NOTT', o dolce tempo benchè nero,
    (Con pace ogn' opra sempr' al fin assalta)
    Ben ved' e ben intende chi t' esalta ;
    E chi t' onor', ha l' intellett' intero.
Tu mozzi e tronchi ogni stanco pensiero ;
    Chè l' umid' ombra ogni quiet' appalta :
    E dall' infima parte alla più alta
    In sogno spesso porti ov' ire spero.
O ombra del morir, per cui sì ferma
    Ogni miseria l' alma al cor nemica,
    Ultimo delli afflitti e buon rimedio ;
Tu rendi sana nostra carn' inferma,
    Rasciug' i pianti, e posi ogni fatica,
    E furi a chi ben vive ogn' ir' e tedio.

XLIV

THE DEFENCE OF NIGHT

O NIGHT, O sweet though sombre span of time !—
    All things find rest upon their journey's end—
    Whoso hath praised thee, well doth apprehend ;
    And whoso honours thee, hath wisdom's prime.
Our cares thou canst to quietude sublime ;
    For dews and darkness are of peace the friend :
    Often by thee in dreams upborne, I wend
    From earth to heaven, where yet I hope to climb.
Thou shade of Death, through whom the soul at
        length
    Shuns pain and sadness hostile to the heart,
    Whom mourners find their last and sure relief !
Thou dost restore our suffering flesh to strength,
    Driest our tears, assuagest every smart,
    Purging the spirits of the pure from grief.

XLV

Quand' il servo il signior d' aspra catena,
    Senz' altra speme, in carcer tien legato,
    Volge in tal uso el suo misero stato,
    Che libero tornar vorrebbe appena.
E el tigre e 'l serpe ancor l' uso raffrena,
    E 'l fier leon ne' folti boschi nato ;
    E 'l nuovo artista, all' opre affaticato,
    Coll' uso e col sudor doppia suo lena.
Ma 'l foco a tal figura non s' uniscie ;
    Chè se l' umor d' un verde legnio estingie,
    Il freddo vecchio scalda, e po' 'l nutriscie.
E tanto il torna in verde etate e spingie,
    Rinnuova e 'nfiamma, allegra e 'ngiovaniscie,
    C' amor col fiato l' alma e 'l cor gli cingie.
        E se motteggia o fingie,
    Chi dice in vecchia etate esser vergognia
    Amar cosa divina, è gran menzognia.
          L'anima che non sognia,
    Non pecca amar le cose di natura,
    Usando peso, termine e misura.

49

XLV

LOVE FEEDS THE FLAME OF AGE

WHEN masters bind a slave with cruel chain,
    And keep him hope-forlorn in bondage pent,
    Use tames his temper to imprisonment,
    And hardly would he fain be free again.
Use curbs the snake and tiger, and doth train
    Fierce woodland lions to bear chastisement :
    And the young artist, all with toil forspent,
    By constant use a giant's strength doth gain.
But with the force of flame it is not so :
    For while fire sucks the sap of the green wood,
    It warms a frore old man and makes him grow ;
With such fine heat of youth and lustihood
    Filling his heart and teaching it to glow,
    That love enfolds him with beatitude,
        If then in playful mood
    He sport and jest, old age need no man blame ;
    For loving things divine implies no shame.
        The soul that knows her aim,
    Sins not by loving God's own counterfeit—
    Due measure kept, and bounds, and order meet.

XLVI

Se da' prim' anni aperto un lento e poco
    Ardor distruggie in breve un verde core ;
    Che farà, chiuso po' da l' ultim' ore,
    D' un più volte arso, un insaziabil foco ?
Se 'l corso di più tempo dà men loco
    A la vita, a le forze e al valore ;
    Che farà a quel che per natura muore
    L' incendio arroto d' amoroso gioco
Farà quel che di me s' aspetta farsi ;
    Cenere al vento sì pietoso e fero,
    C' a' fastidiosi vermi il corpo furi.
Se verde in picciol foco i' piansi e arsi,
    Che più secco ora in un sì grande spero
    Che l' alma al corpo lungo tempo duri ?

XLVI

LOVE'S FLAME DOTH FEED ON AGE

IF some mild heat of love in youth confessed
    Burns a fresh heart with swift consuming fire,
    What will the force be of a flame more dire
    Shut up within an old man's cindery breast ?
If the mere lapse of lengthening years hath pressed
    So sorely that life, strength, and vigour tire,
    How shall he fare who must ere long expire,
    When to old age is added love's unrest ?
Weak as myself, he will be whirled away
    Like dust by winds kind in their cruelty,
    Robbing the loathly worm of its last prey.
A little flame consumed and fed on me
    In my green age : now that the wood is dry,
    What hope against this fire more fierce have I ?

XLVII

Se 'l foco alla bellezza fusse equale
    De' be' vostr' occhi, che da que' si parte,
    Non avria 'l mondo sì gelata parte
    Che non ardesse com' acceso strale.
Ma 'l ciel, pietoso d' ogni nostro male,
    A noi d' ogni beltà, che 'n vo' comparte,
    La visiva virtù toglie e diparte
    Per tranquillar la vita aspra e mortale.
Non è par, dunche, il foco alla beltate ;
    Chè sol di quella parte s' innamora
    Altri del ben del ciel ch' è fra noi inteso.
Così n' avvien, signiore, in questa etate ;
    Se non vi par per voi ch' i' arda e mora,
    Poco conobbi e poco fui acceso.

XLVII

BEAUTY'S INTOLERABLE SPLENDOUR

I<small>F</small> but the fire that lightens in thine eyes
    Were equal with their beauty, all the snow
    And frost of all the world would melt and glow
    Like brands that blaze beneath fierce tropic
        skies.
But heaven in mercy to our miseries
    Dulls and divides the fiery beams that flow
    From thy great loveliness, that we may go
    Through this stern mortal life in tranquil wise.
Thus beauty burns not with consuming rage ;
    For so much only of the heavenly light
    Inflames our love as finds a fervent heart.
This is my case, lady, in sad old age :
    If seeing thee, I do not die outright,
    'Tis that I feel thy beauty but in part.

XLVIII

Se 'l troppo indugio ha più grazia e ventura
    Che per tempo al desir pietà non suole ;
    La mia, negli anni assai, m' affligge e duole :
    Chè 'l gioir vecchio picciol tempo dura.
Contrario ha 'l ciel, se di no' sente o cura,
    Arder nel tempo che ghiacciar si suole,
    Com' io per donna ; onde mie triste e sole
    Lacrime peso con l' età matura.
Ma forse ancor ch' al fin del giorno sia,
    Col sol già quasi oltre all' occaso spento,
    Fra le tenebre folte e 'l freddo rezzo,
S' amor ci infiamma solo a mezza via,
    Nè altrimenti è s' io vecchio ardo drento,
    Donna, tu sol del mio fin fa' 'l mio mezzo.

XLVIII

LOVE'S EVENING

WHAT though long waiting wins more happiness
    Than petulant desire is wont to gain,
    My luck in latest age hath brought me pain,
    Thinking how brief must be an old man's bliss.
Heaven, if it heed our lives, can hardly bless
    This fire of love when frosts are wont to reign :
    For so I love thee, lady, and my strain
    Of tears through age exceeds in tenderness.
Yet peradventure though my day is done,—
    Though nearly past the setting mid thick cloud
    And frozen exhalations sinks my sun,—
If love to only mid-day be allowed,
    And I an old man in my evening burn,
    You, lady, still my night to noon may turn.

XLIX

Dal dolcie pianto al doloroso riso,
　　Da una eterna a una corta pace
　　Caduto son : chè quand' el ver si tace,
　　Soprasta 'l senso a quel da lui diviso.
Nè so se dal mie core o dal tuo viso
　　La colpa vien del mal, che men dispiace
　　Quante più crescie, o dall' ardente face
　　De gli occhi tuo' rubati al paradiso.
La tuo beltà non è cosa mortale,
　　Ma fatta su dal ciel fra noi divina ;
　　Ond' io perdendo ardendo mi conforto,
C' appresso a te non esser posso tale.
　　Se l' arme il ciel del mie morir destina,
　　Chi può, s' i' muoio, dir c' abbiate il torto ?

XLIX

LOVE'S EXCUSE

FROM happy tears to woeful smiles, from peace
    Eternal to a brief and hollow truce,
    How have I fallen !—when 'tis truth we lose,
    Sense triumphs o'er all adverse impulses.
I know not if my heart bred this disease,
    That still more pleasing grows with growing use ;
    Or else thy face, thine eyes, which stole the hues
    And fires of Paradise—less fair than these.
Thy beauty is no mortal thing ; 'twas sent
    From heaven on high to make our earth divine :
    Wherefore, though wasting, burning, I'm con-
        tent ;
For in thy sight what could I do but pine ?
    If God himself thus rules my destiny,
    Who, when I die, can lay the blame on thee ?

L

S' i' avessi creduto al primo sguardo
    Di quest' alma fenice al caldo sole
    Rinnovarmi per foco, come suole
    Nell' ultima vecchiezza, ond' io tutt' ardo ;
Qual più veloce cervio o lince o pardo
    Segue 'l suo bene e fuggie quel che dole,
    Agli atti, al riso, all' oneste parole
    Sarie cors' anzi, ond' or son presto e tardo.
Ma perchè più dolermi, po' ch' i' veggio
    Negli occhi di quest' angel lieto e solo
    Mie pace, mie riposo e mie salute ?
Forse che prima sarie stato il peggio
    Vederlo udirlo, s' or di pari a volo
    Seco m' impenna a seguir suo virtute.

L

IN LOVE'S OWN TIME

HAD I but earlier known that from the eyes
  Of that bright soul that fires me like the sun,
  I might have drawn new strength my race to run,
  Burning as burns the phœnix ere it dies ;
Even as the stag or lynx or leopard flies
  To seek his pleasure and his pain to shun,
  Each word, each smile of her would I have won,
  Flying where now sad age all flight denies.
Yet why complain ? For even now I find
  In that glad angel's face, so full of rest,
  Health and content, heart's ease and peace of
    mind.
Perchance I might have been less simply blest,
  Finding her sooner : if 'tis age alone
  That lets me soar with her to seek God's throne.

LI

TORNAMI al tempo allor che lenta e sciolta
    Al cieco ardor m' era la briglia e 'l freno ;
    Rendimi 'l volto angelico sereno,
    Onde fu seco ogni virtù sepolta ;
E' passi spessi e con fatica molta,
    Che son sì lenti a chi è d' anni pieno ;
    Tornami l' acqua e 'l foco in mezzo il seno,
    Se vuo' di me saziarti un' altra volta.
E s' egli è pur, amor, che tu sol viva
    De' dolci amari pianti de' mortali,
    D' un vecchio stanco oma' puo' goder poco ;
Chè l' alma, quasi giunta all' altra riva,
    Fa scudo a tuo' con più pietosi strali :
    E d' un legni' arso fa vil pruova il foco.

LI

LOVE IN YOUTH AND AGE

BRING back the time when blind desire ran free
  With bit and rein too loose to curb his flight ;
  Give back the buried face, once angel-bright,
  That hides in earth all comely things from me ;
Bring back those journeys ta'en so toilsomely,
  So toilsome-slow to one whose hairs are white ;
  Those tears and flames that in one breast unite ;
  If thou wilt once more take thy fill of me !
Yet Love ! Suppose it true that thou dost thrive
  Only on bitter honey-dews of tears,
  Small profit hast thou of a weak old man.
My soul that toward the other shore doth strive,
  Wards off thy darts with shafts of holier fears ;
  And fire feeds ill on brands no breath can fan.

LI

Tornami al tempo allor che lieta e sciolta
    Al dolce ardor m' era la briglia e 'l freno ;
    Rendimi l' acqua e 'l foco in mezzo il seno,
    Se vuo' ch' i' arda e pianga un' altra volta ;
E' passi spessi e con fatica molta,
    Che son sì lenti a chi è d' anni pieno ;
    Rendimi il volto angelico e sereno,
    Onde a natura ogni virtù fu tolta.
Duro m' è, amor, seguir più le tue ali :
    Cangiato ha nido ; è, se ben mi ricorda,
    Più non beato il buon desir soggiorna.
Rimetti all' arco i tuo' dorati strali ;
    E se morte a pietà non fie più sorda,
    Gran danni obblia chi felice ritorna.

LI

LOVE IN YOUTH AND AGE

BRING back the time when glad desire ran free
    With bit and rein too loose to curb his flight,
    The tears and flames that in one breast unite,
    If thou art fain once more to conquer me !
Bring back those journeys ta'en so toilsomely,
    So toilsome-slow to him whose hairs are white !
    Give back the buried face once angel-bright,
    That taxed all Nature's art and industry.
O Love ! an old man finds it hard to chase
    Thy flying pinions !   Thou hast left thy nest ;
    Nor is my heart as light as heretofore.
Put thy gold arrows to the string once more :
    Then, if Death hear my prayer and grant me
        grace,
    My grief I shall forget, again made blest.

LII

Non vider gli occhi miei cosa mortale
    Allor che ne' bei vostri intera pace
    Trovai ; ma dentro, ov' ogni mal dispiace,
    Chi d' amor l' alma a sè simil m' assale.
E se creata a Dio non fusse eguale,
    Altro che 'l bel di fuor, ch' agli occhi piace,
    Più non vorria ; ma perch' è sì fallace,
    Trascende nella forma più universale.
Io dico, ch' a chi vive quel che muore
    Quetar non può disir ; nè par s' aspetti
    L' eterno al tempo, ove altri cangia il pelo.
Voglia sfrenata el senso è, non amore,
    Che l' alma uccide ; e 'l nostro fa perfetti
    Gli amici qui, ma più per morte in cielo.

LII

CELESTIAL LOVE

I SAW no mortal beauty with these eyes
    When perfect peace in thy fair eyes I found ;
    But far within, where all is holy ground,
    My soul felt Love, her comrade of the skies :
For she was born with God in Paradise ;
    Else should we still to transient loves be bound ;
    But, finding these so false, we pass beyond
    Unto the Love of Loves that never dies.
Nay, things that die, cannot assuage the thirst
    Of souls undying ; nor Eternity
    Serves Time, where all must fade that flourisheth.
Sense is not love, but lawlessness accurst :
    This kills the soul ; while our love lifts on high
    Our friends on earth—higher in heaven through
        death.

LIII

Non è sempre di colpa aspra e mortale
 D' una immensa bellezza un fero ardore,
 Se poi si lascia liquefatto il core,
 Che 'n breve il pènetri un divino strale.
Amore isveglia e desta e impenna l' ale,
 Nè l' alto vol prescrive al van furore ;
 Qual primo grado, ch' al suo creatore,
 Di quel non sazia, l' alma ascende e sale.
L' amor di quel ch' io parlo in alto aspira ;
 Donna, è dissimil troppo ; e mal conviensi
 Arder di quella al cor saggio e virile,
L' un tira al cielo, e l' altro in terra tira ;
 Nell' alma l' un, l' altro abita ne' sensi,
 E l' arco tira a cose basse e vile.

LIII

CELESTIAL AND EARTHLY LOVE

Love is not always harsh and deadly sin :
     If it be love of loveliness divine,
     It leaves the heart all soft and infantine
     For rays of God's own grace to enter in.
Love fits the soul with wings, and bids her win
     Her flight aloft nor e'er to earth decline ;
     'Tis the first step that leads her to the shrine
     Of Him who slakes the thirst that burns within.
The love of that whereof I speak, ascends :
     Woman is different far ; the love of her
     But ill befits a heart all manly wise.
The one love soars, the other downward tends ;
     The soul lights this, while that the senses stir,
     And still his arrow at base quarry flies.

LIV

Veggio nel tuo bel viso, signior mio,
    Quel che narrar mal puossi in questa vita :
    L' anima, della carne ancor vestita,
    Con esso è già più volte asciesa a Dio.
E se 'l vulgo malvagio isciocco e rio
    Di quel che sente, altrui segnia e addita ;
    Non è l' intensa voglia men gradita,
    L' amor, la fede e l' onesto desio.
A quel pietoso fonte, onde siàn tutti,
    S' assembra ogni beltà che qua si vede,
    Più c' altra cosa, alle persone accorte ;
Nè altro saggio abbiàn nè altri frutti
    Del cielo in terra : e s' i' v' amo con fede,
    Trascendo a Dio, e fo dolce la morte.

LIV

LOVE LIFTS TO GOD

From thy fair face I learn, O my loved lord,
    That which no mortal tongue can rightly say ;
    The soul, imprisoned in her house of clay,
    Holpen by thee to God hath often soared :
And though the vulgar, vain, malignant horde
    Attribute what their grosser wills obey,
    Yet shall this fervent homage that I pay,
    This love, this faith, pure joys for us afford.
Lo, all the lovely things we find on earth,
    Resemble for the soul that rightly sees,
    That source of bliss divine which gave us birth :
Nor have we first-fruits or remembrances
    Of heaven elsewhere.   Thus, loving loyally,
    I rise to God and make death sweet by thee.

Tu sa' ch' io so, signior mie, che tu sai
   Ch' i' venni per goderti più da presso ;
   E sai ch' i' so, che tu sa' ch' i' son desso.
   A che più indugio a salutarci omai ?
Se vera è la speranza che mi dài,
   Se vero è 'l buon desio che m' è concesso,
   Rompasi il mur frall' uno e l' altro messo ;
   Chè doppia forza hann' i celati guai.
S' i' amo sol di te, signior mie caro,
   Quel che di te più ami, non ti sdegni ;
   Che l' un dell' altro spirto s' innamora.
Quel che nel tuo bel volto bramo e 'mparo,
   E mal compres' è degli umani ingegni,
   Chi 'l vuol veder, convien che prima mora.

LV

LOVE'S ENTREATY

Thou knowest, love, I know that thou dost know
 That I am here more near to thee to be,
 And knowest that I know thou knowest me :
 What means it then that we are sundered so ?
If they are true, these hopes that from thee flow,
 If it is real, this sweet expectancy,
 Break down the wall that stands 'twixt me and
  thee ;
 For pain in prison pent hath double woe.
Because in thee I love, O my loved lord,
 What thou best lovest, be not therefore stern :
 Souls burn for souls, spirits to spirits cry !
I seek the splendour in thy fair face stored ;
 Yet living man that beauty scarce can learn,
 And he who fain would find it, first must die.

LVI

PER ritornar là donde venne fora,
    L' immortal forma al tuo carcer terreno
    Venne com' angel di pietà sì pieno
    Che sana ogn' intelletto, e 'l mondo onora.
Questo sol m' arde, e questo m' innamora ;
    Non pur di fora il tuo volto sereno :
    Ch' amor non già di cosa che vien meno
    Tien ferma speme, in cu' virtù dimora.
Nè altro avvien di cose altere e nuove
    In cui si preme la natura ; e 'l cielo
    È ch' a lor parto largo s' apparecchia.
Nè Dio, suo grazia, mi mostra altrove,
    Più che 'n alcun leggiadro e mortal velo ;
    E quel sol amo, perchè 'n quel si specchia.

LVI

(FIRST READING)

HEAVEN-BORN BEAUTY

As one who will reseek her home of light,
 Thy form immortal to this prison-house
 Descended, like an angel piteous,
 To heal all hearts and make the whole world
  bright.
'Tis this that thralls my soul in love's delight,
 Not thy clear face of beauty glorious ;
 For he who harbours virtue, still will choose
 To love what neither years nor death can blight.
So fares it ever with things high and rare
 Wrought in the sweat of nature ; heaven above
 Showers on their birth the blessings of her
  prime :
Nor hath God deigned to show Himself elsewhere
 More clearly than in human forms sublime ;
 Which, since they image Him, alone I love.

LVI

VENNE, non so ben donde, ma di fora
  Quell' immortal che del tuo sacro seno
  Non parte, e cerca l' universo appieno,
  E sana ogn' intelletto, e 'l cielo onora,
Questo sol m' arde, e questo m' innamora,
  Non pur di fuora il tuo volto sereno ;
  Ch' amor non già di cosa che vien meno
  Tien ferma speme, in cui virtù dimora.
E se tal forma, per bellezze nuove,
  Trasse dal parto a sè simil fattura ;
  Per vagina di fuor veggio 'l coltello.
Per amar, Dio più non si mostra altrove ;
  Onde gareggia il ciel con la natura,
  Nel casto amarti, da chi più sie bello.

LVI

HEAVEN-BORN BEAUTY

It came, I know not whence, from far above,
  That clear immortal flame that still doth rise
  Within thy sacred breast, and fills the skies,
  And heals all hearts, and adds to heaven new
      love.
This burns me, this, and the pure light thereof ;
  Not thy fair face, thy sweet untroubled eyes :
  For love that is not love for aught that dies,
  Dwells in the soul where no base passions move.
If then such loveliness upon its own
  Should graft new beauties in a mortal birth,
  The sheath bespeaks the shining blade within.
To gain our love God hath not clearer shown
  Himself elsewhere : thus heaven doth vie with
      earth
  To make thee worthy worship without sin.

LVII

PASSA per gli occhi al core in un momento
  Qualunque obbietto di beltà lor sia ;
  E per sì piana, aperta e larga via,
  Ch' a mille non si serra, non che a cento,
D' ogni sorte e fortuna : ond' io pavento,
  Carco d' errore, e più di gelosia ;
  Nè so fra mortal volti qual si sia
  Che 'l desir fermi a sì breve contento,
Che non trascenda al ciel. Ma s' alcun vive
  Error di foco ; di che 'l mondo è pieno,
  Come ch' il fugga, a quel per viver dato ;
Se grazie non ascende all' alte e dive
  Bellezze i buon desir ch' eletti sieno ;
  O che miseria è dunque l' esser nato.

LVII

(FIRST READING)

CARNAL AND SPIRITUAL LOVE

SWIFT through the eyes unto the heart within
    All lovely forms that thrall our spirit stray ;
    So smooth and broad and open is the way
    That thousands and not hundreds enter in.
Burdened with scruples and weighed down with sin,
    These mortal beauties fill me with dismay ;
    Nor find I one that doth not strive to stay
    My soul on transient joy, or lets me win
The heaven I yearn for.   Lo, when erring love—
    Who fills the world, howe'er his power we shun,
    Else were the world a grave and we undone—
Assails the soul, if grace refuse to fan
    Our purged desires and make them soar above,
    What grief it were to have been born a man !

LVII

PASSA per gli occhi al core in un momento
    Qualunque obbietto di beltà lor sia ;
    E per sì larga a sì capace via,
    Ch' a mille non si chiude, non ch' a cento,
D' ogni età d' ogni sesso : ond' io pavento,
    Carco d' affanni, e più di gelosia ;
    Nè fra sì rari volti so qual sia
    Ch' anzi morte mi die 'ntero contento.
S' un ardente desir mortal bellezza
    Ferma del tutto, non discese insieme
    Dal ciel con l' alma, è dunque umana voglia :
Ma se pass 'oltre, amor tuo non me sprezza,
    Ch' altro die cerca ; e di quel più non teme
    Ch' a lato vien contro a sì bassa spoglia.

LVII

(SECOND READING)
CARNAL AND SPIRITUAL LOVE

SWIFT through the eyes unto the heart within
 All lovely forms that thrall our spirit stray ;
 So smooth and broad and open is the way
 That thousands and not hundreds enter in
Of every age and sex : whence I begin,
 Burdened with griefs, but more with dull dis-
  may
 To fear ; nor find mid all their bright array
 One that with full content my heart may win.
If mortal beauty be the food of love,
 It came not with the soul from heaven, and thus
 That love itself must be a mortal fire :
But if love reach to nobler hopes above,
 Thy love shall scorn me not nor dread desire
 That seeks a carnal prey assailing us.

LVIII

Ognor che l' idol mio si rappresenta
    Agli occhi del mio cor debile e forte,
    Fra l' uno e l' altro obbietto entra la morte,
    E più 'l discaccia se più mi spaventa.
L' alma di tale oltraggio esser contenta
    Più spera, che gioir d' ogni altra sorte :
    L' invitto amor con più verace scorte
    A sua difesa s' arma e s' argomenta.
Morir, dice, si può sol una volta ;
    Nè più si nasce : e quel che fuoco muore,
    Che fie po', s' anzi morte in me soggiorna ?
L' acceso amor, donde vien l' alma sciolta,
    S' è calamita d' ogni ardenti core,
    Com' or purgata in foco, a Dio si torna.

LVIII

LOVE AND DEATH

WHENE'ER the idol of these eyes appears
    Unto my musing heart so weak and strong,
    Death comes between her and my soul ere long
    Chasing her thence with troops of gathering
        fears.
Nathless this violence my spirit cheers
    With better hope than if she had no wrong ;
    While Love invincible arrays the throng
    Of dauntless thoughts, and thus harangues his
        peers :
But once, he argues, can a mortal die ;
    But once be born ; and he who dies afire,
    What shall he gain if erst he dwelt with me ?
That burning love whereby the soul flies free,
    Doth lure each fervent spirit to aspire
    Like gold refined in flame to God on high.

LIX

Non più che 'l foco il fabbro il ferro istende
    Al concetto suo caro e bel lavoro ;
    Nè senza foco alcuno artista l' oro
    Al sommo grado suo raffina e rende :
Nè l' unica fenice se riprende,
    Se non prim' arsa.   Ond' io, s' ardendo moro,
    Spero più chiar resurger tra coloro
    Che morte accrescie, e 'l tempo non offende.
Del foco di ch' i' parlo ho gran ventura
    C' ancor per rinnovarmi abb' in me loco,
    Sendo già quasi infra 'l numer de' morti.
O ver s' al cielo asciende per natura
    Al suo elemento, e ch' io converso in foco
    Sie, come fie che seco non mi porti ?

LIX

LOVE IS A REFINER'S FIRE

It is with fire that blacksmiths iron subdue
    Unto fair form, the image of their thought :
    Nor without fire hath any artist wrought
    Gold to its utmost purity of hue.
Nay, nor the unmatched phœnix lives anew,
    Unless she burn : if then I am distraught
    By fire, I may to better life be brought
    Like those whom death restores nor years undo.
The fire whereof I speak, is my great cheer ;
    Such power it hath to renovate and raise
    Me who was almost numbered with the dead ;
And since by nature fire doth find its sphere
    Soaring aloft, and I am all ablaze,
    Heavenward with it my flight must needs be
        sped.

LX

Ben può talor col mio ardente desio
    Salir la speme, e non esser fallace ;
    Chè s' ogni nostro affetto al ciel dispiace,
    A che fin fatto avrebbe il mondo Dio ?
Qual più giusta cagion dell' amarti io
    È, che dar gloria a quell' eterna pace
    Onde pende il divin che di te piace,
    E ch' ogni cor gentil fa casto e pio ?
Fallace speme ha sol l' amor, che muore
    Con la beltà ch' ogni momento scema,
    Ond' è suggetta al variar d' un bel viso.
Dolce è ben quella in un pudico core
    Che per cangiar di scorza o d' ora estrema
    Non manca, e qui caparra il paradiso.

LX

(FIRST READING)
LOVE'S JUSTIFICATION

SOMETIMES my love I dare to entertain
　　With soaring hope not over-credulous ;
　　Since if all human loves were impious,
　　Unto what end did God the world ordain ?
For loving thee what license is more plain
　　Than that I praise thereby the glorious
　　Source of all joys divine, that comfort us
　　In thee, and with chaste fires our soul sustain ?
False hope belongs unto that love alone
　　Which with declining beauty wanes and dies,
　　And, like the face it worships, fades away.
That hope is true which the pure heart hath known,
　　Which alters not with time or death's decay,
　　Yielding on earth earnest of Paradise.

LX

BEN può talor col casto e buon desio
　　Di par la speme, e non esser fallace ;
　　Ch' ogni affetto fra noi s' al ciel dispiace,
　　A che fin fatto arebbe il mondo Iddio ?
S' i' t' amo e reverisco, o signor mio,
　　Anzi s' i' ardo, è per divina pace
　　Che ne' begli occhi tuoi s' alberga e giace,
　　Nimica e schiva d' ogni pensier rio.
Non è amor quel che qui nasce e muore
　　Con la beltà ch' ogni momento scema,
　　Ond' è suggetto al cangiar d' un bel viso :
Ma quello è ben, che 'n pudico core
　　Nè per cangiar di scorza o d' ora estrema
　　Non manca, e qui caparra il paradiso.

LX

LOVE'S JUSTIFICATION

It must be right sometimes to entertain
    Chaste love with hope not over-credulous ;
    Since if all human loves were impious,
    Unto what end did God the world ordain ?
If I love thee and bend beneath thy reign,
    'Tis for the sake of beauty glorious
    Which in thine eyes divine is stored for us,
    And drives all evil thought from its domain.
That is not love whose tyranny we own
    In loveliness that every moment dies ;
    Which, like the face it worships, fades away :
True love is that which the pure heart hath known,
    Which alters not with time or death's decay,
    Yielding on earth earnest of Paradise.

LXI

IN MORTE DI VITTORIA COLONNA

[1547]

Se 'l mie rozzo martello i' duri sassi
    Forma d' uman aspetto or questo or quello,
    Dal ministro, ch' el guida iscorgie e tiello,
    Prendendo il moto, va con gli altrui passi ;
Ma quel divin, ch' in cielo alberga e stassi
    Altri, e sè più, col proprio andar fa bello ;
    E se nessun martel senza martello
    Si può far, da quel vivo ogni altro fassi.
E perchè 'l colpo è di valor più pieno
    Quant' alza più se stesso alla fucina
    Sopra 'l mie, questo al ciel n' è gito a volo.
Onde a me non finito verrà meno,
    S' or non gli dà la fabbrica divina
    Aiuto a farlo, c' al mondo era solo.

LXI

After the Death of Vittoria Colonna

IRREPARABLE LOSS

When my rude hammer to the stubborn stone
    Gives human shape, now that, now this, at will,
    Following his hand who wields and guides it still,
    It moves upon another's feet alone :
But that which dwells in heaven, the world doth fill
    With beauty by pure motions of its own ;
    And since tools fashion tools which else were
        none,
    Its life makes all that lives with living skill.
Now, for that every stroke excels the more
    The higher at the forge it doth ascend,
    Her soul that fashioned mine hath sought the
        skies :
Wherefore unfinished I must meet my end,
    If God, the great artificer, denies
    That aid which was unique on earth before.

69

LXII

IN MORTE DELLA MEDESIMA

Quand' el ministro de' sospir me' tanti
    Al mondo, agli occhi mei, a sè si tolse ;
    Natura, che fra noi degnar lo volse,
    Restò in vergognia, e chi lo vide in pianti.
Ma non come degli altri oggi si vanti
    Del sol del sol, ch' allor ci spense e tolse,
    Morte, c' amor ne vinse, e farlo il tolse
    In terra vivo e 'n ciel fra gli altri santi.
Così credette morte iniqua e rea
    Finir il suon delle virtute sparte,
    E l' alma che men bella esser potea.
Contrari effetti alluminan le carte
    Di vita più che 'n vita non solea,
    E morta ha 'l ciel, c' allor non avea parte.

LXII

LOVE'S TRIUMPH OVER DEATH

When she who was the source of all my sighs,
  Fled from the world, herself, my straining sight,
  Nature who gave us that unique delight,
  Was sunk in shame, and we had weeping eyes.
Yet shall not vauntful Death enjoy this prize,
  This sun of suns which then he veiled in night ;
  For Love hath triumphed, lifting up her light
  On earth and mid the saints in Paradise.
What though remorseless and impiteous doom
  Deemed that the music of her deeds would die,
  And that her splendour would be sunk in gloom,
The poet's page exalts her to the sky
  With life more living in the lifeless tomb,
  And death translates her soul to reign on high.

LXIII

IN MORTE DELLA MEDESIMA

Be' mi dove' con si felice sorte,
    Mentre che Febo il poggio tutto ardea,
    Levar da terra, allor quand' io potea
    Con le sue penne, e far dolce la morte.
Or m' è sparito ; e se 'l fuggir men forte
    De' giorni lieti invan mi promettea,
    Ragion' è ben ch' all' alma ingrata e rea
    L' etade manchi, e 'l ciel chiugga le porte.
Le penne mi furn' ale, e 'l poggio scale,
    Febo lucerna a' piè ; nè m' era allora
    Men salute il morir, che maraviglia.
Morendo or senza, al ciel l' alma non sale ;
    Nè di lor la memoria il cor ristora :
    Chè tardi, e doppo il danno, chi consiglia ?

LXIII

AFTER THE DEATH OF VITTORIA COLONNA

AFTER SUNSET

WELL might I in those days so fortunate,
   What time the sun lightened my path above,
   Have soared from earth to heaven, raised by
      her love
   Who winged my labouring soul and sweetened
      fate.
That sun hath set ; and I with hope elate
   Who deemed that those bright days would never
      move,
   Find that my thankless soul deprived thereof,
   Declines to death, while heaven still bars the
      gate.
Love lent me wings ; my path was like a stair ;
   A lamp unto my feet, that sun was given ;
   And death was safety and great joy to find.
But dying now, I shall not climb to heaven ;
   Nor can mere memory cheer my heart's de-
      spair :—
   What help remains when hope is left behind ?

LXIV

IN MORTE DELLA MEDESIMA

Qual maraviglia è se prossimo al foco
  Mi strussi e arsi, se or ch' egli è spento
  Di fuor, m' affligge e mi consumo drento,
  E 'n cener mi riduce a poco a poco ?
Vedea ardendo sì lucente il loco
  Onde pendea il mio greve tormento,
  Che sol la vista mi facea contento ;
  E morte e strazi m' eran festa e gioco.
Ma po' che del gran foco lo splendore,
  Che m' ardeva e nutriva, il ciel m' invola,
  Un carbon resto acceso e ricoperto.
E s' altre legne non mi porge amore
  Che lievin fiamma, una favilla sola
  Non fie di me, sì 'n cener mi converto.

LXIV

A WASTED BRAND

If being near the fire I burned with it,
>   Now that its flame is quenched and doth not
>   show,
>   What wonder if I waste within and glow,
>   Dwindling away to cinders bit by bit ?
While still it burned, I saw so brightly lit
>   That splendour whence I drew my grievous woe,
>   That from its sight alone could pleasure flow,
>   And death and torment both seemed exquisite.
But now that heaven hath robbed me of the blaze
>   Of that great fire which burned and nourished
>   me,
>   A coal that smoulders 'neath the ash am I.
Unless Love furnish wood fresh flames to raise,
>   I shall expire with not one spark to see,
>   So quickly into embers do I die !

LXV

A GIORGIO VASARI

[1554]

Giunto è già 'l corso della vita mia,
 Con tempestoso mar per fragil barca,
 Al comun porto, ov' a render si varca
 Conto e ragion d' ogn' opra trista e pia.
Onde l' affettuosa fantasia,
 Che l' arte mi fece idol' e monarca,
 Conosco or ben quant' era d' error carca,
 E quel ch' a mal suo grado ogn' uom desia.
Gli amorosi pensier, già vani e lieti,
 Che fieno or, s' a duo morte m' avvicino ?
 D' una so 'l certo, e l' altra mi minaccia.
Nè pinger nè scolpir fia più che quieti
 L' anima volta a quell' Amor divino
 Ch' aperse, a prender noi, in croce le braccia.

LXV

To Giorgio Vasari

ON THE BRINK OF DEATH

Now hath my life across a stormy sea
 Like a frail bark reached that wide port where
  all
 Are bidden, ere the final reckoning fall
 Of good and evil for eternity.
Now know I well how that fond phantasy
 Which made my soul the worshipper and thrall
 Of earthly art, is vain ; how criminal
 Is that which all men seek unwillingly.
Those amorous thoughts which were so lightly dressed,
 What are they when the double death is nigh ?
 The one I know for sure, the other dread.
Painting nor sculpture now can lull to rest
 My soul that turns to His great love on high,
 Whose arms to clasp us on the cross were spread.

73

LXVI

Le favole del mondo m' hanno tolto
    Il tempo dato a contemplare Iddio ;
    Nè sol le grazie suo poste in oblio,
    Ma con lor, più che senza, a peccar volto.
Quel c' altri saggio, me fa cieco e stolto,
    E tardi a riconoscer l' error mio.
    Scema la speme, e pur crescie 'l desio
    Che da te sie dal propio amor disciolto.
Ammezzami la strada c' al ciel sale,
    Signior mie caro, e a quel mezzo solo
    Salir m' è di bisognio la tuo 'ita.
Mettimi in odio quante 'l mondo vale,
    E quanto suo bellezze onoro e colo,
    C' anzi morte caparri eterna vita.

LXVI

VANITY OF VANITIES

THE fables of the world have filched away
    The time I had for thinking upon God ;
    His grace lies buried 'neath oblivion's sod,
    Whence springs an evil crop of sins alway.
What makes another wise, leads me astray,
    Slow to discern the bad path I have trod :
    Hope fades ; but still desire ascends that God
    May free me from self-love, my sure decay.
Shorten half-way my road to heaven from earth !
    Dear Lord, I cannot even half-way rise,
    Unless Thou help me on this pilgrimage.
Teach me to hate the world so little worth,
    And all the lovely things I clasp and prize ;
    That endless life, ere death, may be my wage.

LXVII

Non è più bassa o vil cosa terrena
    Che quel che, senza te, mi sento e sono ;
    Ond' all' alto desir chiede perdono
    La debile mie propia e stanca lena.
Deh porgi, Signor mio, quella catena
    Che seco annoda ogni celeste dono ;
    La fede dico, a che mi stringo e sprono ;
    Nè, mie colpa, n' ho grazia intiera e piena.
Tanto mi fie maggior quant' è più raro
    Il don de' doni ; e maggior fia, se senza,
    Pace e contento il mondo in sè non have.
Po' che non fusti del tuo sangue avaro,
    Che sarà di tal don la tua clemenza,
    Se 'l ciel non s' apre a noi con altra chiave.

LXVII

A PRAYER FOR FAITH

There's not on earth a thing more vile and base
    Than, lacking Thee, I feel myself to be :
    For pardon prays my own debility,
    Yearning in vain to lift me to Thy face.
Stretch to me, Lord, that chain whose links enlace
    All heavenly gifts and all felicity—
    Faith, whereunto I strive perpetually,
    Yet cannot find (my fault) her perfect grace.
That gift of gifts, the rarer 'tis, the more
    I count it great ; more great, because to earth
    Without it neither peace nor joy is given.
If Thou Thy blood so lovingly didst pour,
    Let not that bounty fail or suffer dearth,
    Withholding Faith that opes the doors of heaven.

LXVIII

A MONSIGNOR LODOVICO BECCADELLI
ARCIVESCOVO DI RAGUGIA.   RISPOSTA
[1556]

PER croce e grazia, e per diverse pene,
  Son certo, Monsignor, trovarci in cielo :
  Ma prima ch' a l' estremo ultimo anelo
  Goderci in terra mi parria pur bene.
Se l' aspra via co i monti e co 'l mar tiene
  L' un da l' altro lontan, lo spirto e 'l zelo
  Non cura intoppi di neve o di gielo,
  Nè l' alia del pensier lacci o catene.
Ond' io con esso son sempre con voi,
  E piango e parlo del mio morto Urbino,
  Che vivo or forse saria costà meco,
Com' ebbi già in pensier.   Sua morte poi
  M' affretta e tira per altro camino,
  Dove m' aspetta ad albergar con seco.

76

LXVIII

God's grace, the cross, our troubles multiplied,
    Will make us meet in heaven, full well I know :
    Yet ere we yield our breath, on earth below
    Why need a little solace be denied ?
Though seas and mountains and rough ways divide
    Our feet asunder, neither frost nor snow
    Can make the soul her ancient love forgo ;
    Nor chains nor bonds the wings of thought
        have tied.
Borne by these wings with thee I dwell for aye,
    And weep, and of my dead Urbino talk,
    Who, were he living, now perchance would be,
For so 'twas planned, thy guest as well as I :
    Warned by his death another way I walk
    To meet him where he waits to live with me.

LXIX

Di morte certo, ma non già dell' ora ;
 La vita è breve, e poco me n' avanza ;
 Diletta al senso è non però la stanza
 A l' alma, che mi priega pur ch' i' mora.
Il mondo è cieco, e 'l tristo esempio ancora
 Vince e sommerge ogni perfetta usanza ;
 Spent' è la luce, e seco ogni baldanza ;
 Trimfa il falso, e 'l ver non surge fora.
Deh quando fie, Signor, quel che s' aspetta
 Per chi ti crede ? ch' ogni troppo indugio
 Tronca la speme, e l' alma fa mortale.
Che val che tanto lume altrui prometta,
 S' anzi vien morte, e senz' alcun' refugio
 Ferma per sempre in che stato altri assale ?

LXIX

WAITING FOR DEATH

My death must come ; but when, I do not know :
    Life's short, and little life remains for me :
    Fain would my flesh abide ; my soul would flee
Heavenward, for still she calls on me to go.
Blind is the world ; and evil here below
    O'erwhelms and triumphs over honesty :
    The light is quenched ; quenched too is bravery :
Lies reign, and truth hath ceased her face to show.
When will that day dawn, Lord, for which he waits
    Who trusts in Thee ?   Lo, this prolonged delay
    Destroys all hope and robs the soul of life.
Why streams the light from those celestial gates,
    If death prevent the day of grace, and stay
    Our souls for ever in the toils of strife ?

LXX

Carico d' anni e di peccati pieno,
    E col tristo uso radicato e forte,
    Vicin mi veggio a l' una e l' altra morte,
    E parte 'l cor nutrisco di veleno.
Nè propie forze ho, c' al bisogno sieno
    Per cangiar vita, amor, costume o sorte,
    Senza le tuo divine e chiare scorte,
    Più che da noi, per noi guida e freno.
Non basta, Signor mio, che tu m' invogli
    Di ritornar là dove l' alma sia,
    Non come prima di nulla, creata.
Anzi che del mortal la privi e spogli,
    Prego m' ammezzi l' alta e erta via
    E fie più chiara e certa la tornata.

LXX

A PRAYER FOR STRENGTH

Burdened with years and full of sinfulness,
    With evil custom grown inveterate,
    Both deaths I dread that close before me wait,
    Yet feed my heart on poisonous thoughts no less.
No strength I find in mine own feebleness
    To change or life or love or use or fate,
    Unless Thy heavenly guidance come, though
        late,
    Which only helps and stays our nothingness.
'Tis not enough, dear Lord, to make me yearn
    For that celestial home, where yet my soul
    May be new made, and not, as erst, of nought :
Nay, ere Thou strip her mortal vestment, turn
    My steps toward the steep ascent, that whole
    And pure before Thy face she may be brought.

LXXI

Forse perchè d' altrui pietà mi vegnia,
  Perchè dell' altrui colpe più non rida
  Nel mie proprio valor, senz' altra guida,
  Caduta è l' alma che fu già sì' degnia.
Nè so qual militar sott' altra insegnia,
  Non che da vincer, da campar più fida ;
  E che al tumulto dell' averse strida
  Non pera, ove 'l poter tuo non sostegnia.
O carne, o sangue, o legnio, o doglia strema,
  Giusto per vo' si facci el mie peccato,
  Di ch' i' pur naqqui, e tal fu 'l padre mio.
Tu sol se' buon : la tuo pietà suprema
  Soccorra al mie preditto iniquo stato ;
  Sì presso a morte, e sì lontan da Dio.

LXXI

A PRAYER FOR PURIFICATION

PERCHANCE that I might learn what pity is,
    That I might laugh at erring men no more,
    Secure in my own strength as heretofore,
    My soul hath fallen from her state of bliss :
Nor know I under any flag but this
    How fighting I may 'scape those perils sore,
    Or how survive the rout and horrid roar
    Of adverse hosts, if I Thy succour miss.
O flesh ! O blood ! O cross ! O pain extreme !
    By you may those foul sins be purified,
    Wherein my fathers were, and I was born !
Lo, Thou alone art good ! let Thy supreme
    Pity my state of evil cleanse and hide—
    So near to death, so far from God, forlorn.

LXXII

DEH fammiti vedere in ogni loco !
　　Se da mortal bellezza arder mi sento,
　　A presso al tuo mi sarà foco ispento,
　　E io nel tuo sarò, com' ero, in foco.
Signor mie caro, i' te sol chiamo e 'nvoco
　　Contro l' inutil mie cieco tormento :
　　Tu sol puo' rinnovarmi fuora e drento
　　Le voglie, e 'l senno, e 'l valor lento e poco.
Tu desti al tempo ancor quest' alma diva,
　　E 'n questa spoglia ancor fragil' e stanca
　　L' incarcerasti, e con fiero destino.
Che poss' io altro, che così non viva ?
　　Ogni ben senza te, Signor, mi manca.
　　Il cangiar sorte è sol poter divino.

LXXII

A PRAYER FOR AID

Oh, make me see Thee, Lord, where'er I go !
  If mortal beauty sets my soul on fire,
  That flame when near to Thine must needs
      expire,
  And I with love of only Thee shall glow.
Dear Lord, Thy help I seek against this woe,
  These torments that my spirit vex and tire ;
  Thou only with new strength canst re-inspire
  My will, my sense, my courage faint and low.
Thou gavest me on earth this soul divine ;
  And Thou within this body weak and frail
  Didst prison it—how sadly there to live !
How can I make its lot less vile than mine ?
  Without Thee, Lord, all goodness seems to fail.
  To alter fate is God's prerogative.

LXXIII

SCARCO d' un' importuna e grave salma,
  Signor mio caro, e dal mondo disciolto,
  Qual fragil legno, a te stanco mi volto
  Dall' orribil procella in dolce calma.
Le spine, e' chiodi, e l' un e l' altra palma
  Col tuo benigno umil pietoso volto
  Prometton grazia di pentirsi molto,
  E speme di salute alla trist' alma.
Non mirin con giustizia i tuoi santi occhi
  Il mio passato, e 'l gastigato orecchio
  Non tenda a quello il tuo braccio severo.
Tuo sangue sol mie colpe lavi e tocchi,
  E più abbondi, quant' io son più vecchio,
  Di pront' aita e di perdon' intero.

LXXIII

AT THE FOOT OF THE CROSS

Freed from a burden sore and grievous band,
   Dear Lord, and from this wearying world untied,
   Like a frail bark I turn me to Thy side,
   As from a fierce storm to a tranquil land.
Thy thorns, Thy nails, and either bleeding hand,
   With Thy mild gentle piteous face, provide
   Promise of help and mercies multiplied,
   And hope that yet my soul secure may stand.
Let not Thy holy eyes be just to see
   My evil past, Thy chastened ears to hear
   And stretch the arm of judgment to my crime :
Let Thy blood only lave and succour me,
   Yielding more perfect pardon, better cheer,
   As older still I grow with lengthening time.

LXXIV

S' AVVIEN che spesso il gran desir prometta
    A' miei tanti' anni dimolti anni ancora,
    Non fa che morte non s' appressi ognora ;
    E là dove men duol, manco s' affretta.
A che più vita per gioir s' aspetta,
    Se sol nella miseria Iddio s' adora ?
    Lieta fortuna, e con lunga dimora,
    Tanto più nuoce quanto più diletta.
E se talor, tuo grazia, il cor m' assale,
    Signor mio caro, quello ardente zelo
    Che l' anima conforta e rassicura,
Da che 'l proprio valor nulla mi vale,
    Subito allor sarie da girne in cielo :
    Chè con più tempo il buon voler men dura.

LXXIV

(FIRST READING)

A PRAYER FOR GRACE IN DEATH

WHAT though strong love of life doth flatter me
    With hope of yet more years on earth to stay,
    Death none the less draws nearer day by day,
    Who to sad souls alone comes lingeringly.
Yet why desire long life and jollity,
    If in our griefs alone to God we pray ?
    Glad fortune, length of days, and pleasure slay
    The soul that trusts to their felicity.
Then if at any hour through grace divine
    The fiery shafts of love and faith that cheer
    And fortify the soul, my heart assail,
Since nought achieve these mortal powers of mine,
    Straight may I wing my way to heaven ; for here
    With lengthening days good thoughts and
        wishes fail.

LXXIV

PARMI che spesso un gran desir prometta
    A' miei molti anni dimolti anni ancora ;
    Nè manca morte di scemarmi ognora
    Tanto la vita, quanto più diletta.
Che miglior tempo al mio cangiar s' aspetta,
    Se sol nella miseria Iddio s' adora ?
    Deh ! tra' mi, Signor mio, deh ! tra' mi or fora
    D' ogni negozio, che fortuna alletta.
Che se talor, tuo grazia, il cor m' assale
    D' amor di fede quell' ardente zelo,
    Che l' alma ne conforta e rassicura,
Perchè 'l proprio valor nulla mi vale,
    Tu 'l fermi in me sì come spirto in cielo ;
    Chè nessun buon voler senza te dura.

LXXIV

A PRAYER FOR GRACE IN DEATH

OFTTIMES my great desire doth flatter me
    With hope on earth yet many years to stay ;
    Still Death, the more I love it, day by day
    Takes from the life I love so tenderly.
What better time for that dread change could be,
    If in our griefs alone to God we pray ?
    Oh, lead me, Lord, oh, lead me far away
    From every thought that lures my soul from
        Thee !
Yea, if at any hour, through grace of Thine,
    The fervent zeal of love and faith that cheer
    And fortify the soul, my heart assail,
Since nought achieve these mortal powers of mine,
    Plant, like a saint in heaven, that virtue here ;
    For, lacking Thee, all good must faint and fail.

LXXV

Vorrei voler, Signior, quel ch' io non voglio ;
 Tra 'l foco e 'l cor di iaccia un vel s' asconde,
 Che 'l foco ammorza ; onde non corrisponde
 La penna all' opre, e fa bugiardo 'l foglio.
I' t' amo con la lingua, e poi mi doglio ;
 Ch' amor non giungie al cor, nè so ben onde
 Apra l' uscio alla grazia, che s' infonde
 Nel cor, che scacci ogni spietato orgoglio.
Squarcia 'l vel tu, Signior, rompi quel muro
 Che con la suo durezza ne ritarda
 Il sol della tuo luce al mondo spenta.
Manda 'l preditto lume a noi venturo
 Alla tuo bella sposa, accio ch' io arda
 E te senz' alcun dubbio il cor sol senta.

LXXV

HEART-COLDNESS

FAIN would I wish what my heart cannot will :
    Between it and the fire a veil of ice
    Deadens the fire, so that I deal in lies ;
    My words and actions are discordant still.
I love Thee with my tongue, then mourn my fill ;
    For love warms not my heart, nor can I rise,
    Or ope the doors of Grace, who from the skies
    Might flood my soul, and pride and passion kill.
Rend Thou the veil, dear Lord ! Break Thou that
        wall
    Which with its stubbornness retards the rays
    Of that bright sun this earth hath dulled for me !
Send down Thy promised light to cheer and fall
    On Thy fair spouse, that I with love may blaze,
    And, free from doubt, my heart feel only Thee !

LXXVI

Non fur men lieti che turbati e tristi,
 Che tu patissi, e non già lor, la morte,
 Gli spirti eletti, onde le chiuse porte
 Del ciel, di terra a l' uom col sangue apristi.
Lieti ; poichè, creato, il redemisti
 Dal primo error di suo misera sorte :
 Tristi ; a sentir ch' a la pena aspra e forte,
 Servo de' servi in croce divenisti.
Onde e chi fusti il ciel ne diè tal segno,
 Che scurò gli occhi suoi, la terra aperse,
 Tremorono i monti, e torbide fur l' acque ;
Tolse i gran Padri al tenebroso regno,
 Gli angeli brutti in più doglia sommerse :
 Godè sol l' uom, ch' al battesmo rinacque;

LXXVI

THE DEATH OF CHRIST

Nor less elate than smitten with wild woe
    To see not them but Thee by death undone,
    Were those blest souls, when Thou above the
      sun
    Didst raise, by dying, men that lay so low :
Elate, since freedom from all ills that flow
    From their first fault for Adam's race was won ;
    Sore smitten, since in torment fierce God's son
    Served servants on the cruel cross below.
Heaven showed she knew Thee, who Thou wert and
      whence,
    Veiling her eyes above the riven earth ;
    The mountains trembled and the seas were
      troubled.
He took the Fathers from hell's darkness dense :
    The torments of the damnèd fiends redoubled :
    Man only joyed, who gained baptismal birth.

LXXVII

MENTRE m' attrista e duol, parte m' è caro
    Il pensier del passato, s' al cor riede
    Mie miserie e peccati, e ragion chiede
    Del tempo perso, onde non è riparo.
Caro m' è sol, perch' anzi morte imparo
    Quant' ogni uman diletto ha corta fede ;
    Tristo m' è, ch' a trovar grazia e mercede
    Nell' ultim' ora è pur dubioso e raro.
Che, benchè alle promesse tue s' attenda,
    Creder, Signore, è troppo grande ardire
    Ch' ogni gran tardità pietà perdoni.
Ma pur dal tuo sangue si comprenda
    Quanto infinito fu 'l tuo gran martire,
    Senza misura sien tuo' cari doni.

LXXVII

THE BLOOD OF CHRIST

Mid weariness and woe I find some cheer
    In thinking of the past, when I recall
    My weakness and my sins, and reckon all
    The vain expense of days that disappear
This cheers by making, ere I die, more clear
    The frailty of what men delight miscall ;
    But saddens me to think how rarely fall
    God's grace and mercies in life's latest year.
For though Thy promises our faith compel,
    Yet, Lord, what man shall venture to maintain
    That pity will condone our long neglect ?
Still from Thy blood poured forth we know full well
    How without measure was Thy martyr's pain,
    How measureless the gifts we dare expect.

NOTES AND APPENDICES

NOTES

I. p. 2. Quoted by Donato Giannotti in his Dialogue *De' giorni che Dante consumò nel cercare l' Inferno e 'l Purgatorio*. The date of its composition is perhaps 1545.

II. p. 3. Written probably for Donato Giannotti about the same date.

III. p. 4. Belonging to the year 1506, when Michael Angelo quarrelled with Julius and left Rome in anger. The tree referred to in the last line is the oak of the Rovere family.

IV. p. 5. Same date, and same circumstances. The autograph has these words at the foot of the sonnet : *Vostro Miccelangniolo, in Turchia*. Rome itself, the Sacred City, has become a land of infidels.

V. p. 6. Ser Giovanni da Pistoja was Chancellor of the Florentine Academy. The date is probably 1509. The *Sonetto a Coda* is generally humorous or satiric.

VI. p. 7. Written in one of those moments of *affanno* or *stizzo* to which the sculptor was subject.

NOTES

For the old bitterness of feeling between Florence and Pistoja, see Dante, *Inferno*, xxiv., xxv.

VII. p. 8. Michael Angelo was ill during the summer of 1544, and was nursed by Luigi del Riccio in his own house. Shortly after his recovery he quarrelled with his friend, and wrote him this sonnet as well as a very angry letter.

VIII. p. 9. Cecchino Bracci was a boy of rare and surpassing beauty, who died at Rome, January 8, 1544, in his seventeenth year. Besides this sonnet, which refers to a portrait Luigi del Riccio had asked him to make of the dead youth, Michael Angelo composed a series of forty-eight quatrains upon the same subject, and sent them to his friend Luigi. Michelangelo the younger, thinking that " *l' ignoranzia degli uomini ha campo di mormorare*," suppressed the name Cecchino and changed *lui* into *lei*. Date about 1544.

IX. p. 10. Line 4 : " The Archangel's scales alone can weigh my gratitude against your gift." Lines 5–8 : " Your courtesy has taken away all my power of responding to it. I am as helpless as a ship becalmed, or a wisp of straw on a stormy sea."

X. p. 11. Michael Angelo, when asked to make a portrait of his friend's mistress, declares that he is unable to do justice to her beauty. The name *Mancina* is a pun upon the Italian word for the left arm, *Mancino*. This lady was a famous and venal beauty, mentioned among the loves of the poet Molsa.

NOTES

XI. p. 12.   Date, 1550.

XII. p. 13.   This and the three next sonnets may with tolerable certainty be referred to the series written on various occasions for Vittoria Colonna.

XIII. p. 14.   Sent together with a letter, in which we read : *l' aportatore di questa sarà Urbino, che sta meco.* Urbino was M. A.'s old servant, workman, and friend.   See No. LXVIII. and note.

XIV. p. 15.   The thought is that, as the sculptor carves a statue from a rough model by addition and subtraction of the marble, so the lady of his heart refines and perfects his rude native character.

XV. p. 17.   This sonnet is the theme of Varchi's *Lezione.*   There is nothing to prove that it was addressed to Vittoria Colonna.   Varchi calls it " *un suo altissimo sonetto pieno di quella antica purezza e dantesca gravità.*"

XVI. p. 18.   The thought of the fifteenth is repeated with some variations.   His lady's heart holds for the lover good and evil things, according as he has the art to draw them forth.

XVIII. p. 20.   In the terzets he describes the temptations of the artist-nature, over-sensitive to beauty.   Michelangelo the younger so altered these six lines as to destroy the autobiographical allusion. —Cp. No. XXVIII., note.

XIX. p. 21.   The lover's heart is like an intaglio, precious by being inscribed with his lady's image.

XX. p. 22.   An early composition, written on the

back of a letter sent to the sculptor in Bologna by his brother Simone in 1507. M. A. was then working at the bronze statue of Julius II. Who the lady of his love was, we do not know. Notice the absence of Platonic *concetti*.

XXIII. p. 25. It is hardly necessary to call attention to Michael Angelo's oft-recurring Platonism. The thought that the eye alone perceives the celestial beauty, veiled beneath the fleshly form of the beloved, is repeated in many sonnets—especially in XXV., XXVIII.

XXIV. p. 26. Composed probably in the year 1529.

XXV. p. 27. Written on the same sheet as the foregoing sonnet, and composed probably in the same year. The thought is this : beauty passing from the lady into the lover's soul, is there spiritualised and becomes the object of a spiritual love.

XXVII. p. 29. To escape from his lady, either by interposing another image of beauty between the thought of her and his heart, or by flight, is impossible.

XXVIII. p. 30. Compare Madrigal VII. in illustration of lines 5 to 8. By the analogy of that passage, I should venture to render lines 6 and 7 thus :—

> He made thee light, and me the eyes of art
> Nor fails my soul to find God's counterpart.

NOTES

XXX. p. 32. Varchi, quoting this sonnet in his *Lezione*, conjectures that it was composed for Tommaso Cavalieri.

XXXI. p. 33. Varchi asserts without qualification that this sonnet was addressed to Tommaso Cavalieri. The pun in the last line, *Resto prigion d' un Cavalier armato*, seems to me to decide the matter, though Signor Guasti and Signor Gotti both will have it that a woman must have been intended. Michelangelo the younger has only left one line, the second, untouched in his *rifacimento*. Instead of the last words he gives *un cuor di virtù armato*, being over-scrupulous for his great-uncle's reputation.

XXXII. p. 34. Written at the foot of a letter addressed by Giuliano Bugiardini, the painter, from Florence, to M. A. in Rome, August 5, 1532. This, then, is probably the date of the composition.

XXXIV. p. 37. The metaphor of fire, flint, and mortar breaks down in the last line, where M. A. forgets that gold cannot strike a spark from stone.

XXXV. p. 38. Line 9 has the word *Signor*. It is almost certain that where M. A. uses this word without further qualification in a love sonnet, he means his mistress. I have sometimes translated it " heart's lord " or " loved lord," because I did not wish to merge the quaintness of this ancient Tuscan usage in the more commonplace " lady."

XXXVI. p. 39. Line 3 : *the lord, &c.* This again is the poet's mistress. The drift of the sonnet is this : his soul can find no expression but through speech, and speech is too gross to utter the purity of his feeling. His mistress again receives his tongue's message with her ears ; and thus there is an element of sensuality, false and alien to his intention, both in his complaint and in her acceptation of it. The last line is a version of the proverb : *chi è avvezzo a dir bugie, non crede a nessuno.*

XXXVII. p. 40. At the foot of the sonnet is written *Mandato.* The two last lines play on the words *signor* and *signoria.* To whom it was sent we do not know for certain ; but we may conjecture Vittoria Colonna.

XXXIX. p. 42. The paper on which this sonnet is written has a memorandum with the date January 6, 1529. " On my return from Venice, I, Michelagniolo Buonarroti, found in the house about five loads of straw," &c. It belongs therefore to the period of the siege of Florence, when M. A., as is well known, fled for a short space to Venice. In line 12, I have translated *il mie signiore, my lady.*

XL. p. 43. No sonnet in the whole collection seems to have cost M. A. so much trouble as this. Besides the two completed versions, which I have rendered, there are several scores of rejected or various readings for single lines in the MSS. The Platonic doctrine of Anamnesis probably supplies the key to the thought which the poet attempted to work out.

NOTES

XLI., XLII., XLIII., XLIV. pp. 45–48. There is nothing to prove that these four sonnets on Night were composed in sequence. On the contrary, the personal tone of XLI. seems to separate this from the other three. XLIV. may be accepted as a palinode for XLIII.

XLV., XLVI. pp. 49–50. Both sonnets deal half humorously with a thought very prominent in M. A.'s compositions—the effect of love on one who is old in years. Cp. XLVIII., L.

XLVII. p. 51. The Platonic conception that the pure form of Beauty or of Truth, if seen, would be overwhelming in its brilliancy.

XLIX. p. 53. The *dolcie pianto* and *eterna pace* are the tears and peace of piety. The *doloroso riso* and *corta pace* are the smiles and happiness of earthly love.

LII. p. 57. Here is another version of this very beautiful sonnet :—

No mortal thing enthralled these longing eyes
    When perfect peace in thy fair face I found ;
    But far within, where all is holy ground,
    My soul felt Love, her comrade of the skies :
For she was born with God in Paradise ;
    Nor all the shows of beauty shed around
    This fair false world her wings to earth have bound ;
    Unto the Love of Loves aloft she flies.
Nay, things that suffer death, quench not the fire
    Of deathless spirits ; nor eternity
    Serves sordid Time, that withers all things rare.
Not love but lawless impulse is desire :
    That slays the soul ; our love makes still more fair
    Our friends on earth, fairer in death on high.

NOTES

LIII. p. 58. This is the doctrine of the Symposium; the scorn of merely sexual love is also Platonic.

LIV. p. 59. Another sonnet on the theme of the Uranian as distinguished from the Vulgar love. See below, LVI., for a parallel to the second terzet.

LV. p. 60. The date may be 1532. The play on words in the first quatrain and the first terzet is Shakespearian.

LIX. p. 66. Two notes, appended to the two autographs of this sonnet, show that M. A. regarded it as a *jeu d'esprit*. "*Per carnovale par lecito far qualche pazzia a chi non va in maschera.*" "*Questo non è fuoco da carnovale, però vel mando di quaresima; e a voi mi rachomando. Vostro Michelagniolo.*"

LXI. p. 69. Date 1547. No sonnet presents more difficulties than this, in which M. A. has availed himself of a passage in the *Cratylus* of Plato. The divine hammer spoken of in the second couplet is the ideal pattern after which the souls of men are fashioned; and this in the first terzet seems to be identified with Vittoria Colonna. In the second terzet he regards his own soul as imperfect, lacking the final touches which it might have received from hers. See XIV. for a somewhat similar conceit.

LXIV. p. 72. The image is that of a glowing

wood coal smouldering away to embers amid its own ashes.

LXV. p. 73. Date 1554. Addressed *A messer Giorgio Vasari, amico e pittor singulare*, with this letter : *Messer Giorgio, amico caro, voi direte ben ch' io sie vecchio e pazzo a voler far sonetti ; ma perchè molti dicono ch' io son rimbambito, ho voluto far l'uficio mio, ec. A dì 19 di settembre 1554. Vostro Michelagniolo Buonarroti in Roma.*

LXVI., LXVII. pp. 74–75. These two sonnets were sent to Giorgio Vasari in 1555 (?) with this letter : *Messer Giorgio, io vi mando dua sonetti ; e benchè sieno cosa sciocca, il fo perchè veggiate dove io tengo i mie' pensieri : e quando arete ottantuno anni, come ò io, mi crederete. Pregovi gli diate a messer Giovan Francesco Fattucci, che me ne à chiesti. Vostro Michelagniolo Buonarroti in Roma.* The first was also sent to Monsignor Beccadelli, Archbishop of Ragusa, who replied to it. For his sonnet, see Signor Guasti's edition, p. 233.

LXVIII. p. 76. Date 1556. Written in reply to his friend's invitation that he should pay him a visit at Ragusa. Line 10 : this Urbino was M. A.'s old and faithful servant, Francesco d'Amadore di Casteldurante, who lived with him twenty-six years, and died at Rome in 1556.

LXIX.–LXXVII. pp. 77–86. The dates of this series of penitential sonnets are not known. It is clear that they were written in old age. It will be remembered that the latest piece of marble on which Michael Angelo worked, was the unfinished Pietà now standing behind the choir of the Duomo at Florence. Many of his latest drawings are designs for a Crucifixion.

APPENDICES

APPENDIX I

THE *Rivista Europea* of June 1875 publishes an
article by Signor V. de Tivoli concerning an inedited
sonnet of Michael Angelo, which he deciphered
from the Autograph, written upon the back of one
of the original drawings in the Taylor Gallery at
Oxford. This drawing formed part of the Ottley
and Lawrence Collection. It represents horses in
various attitudes, together with a skirmish between
a mounted soldier and a group of men on foot.
Signor de Tivoli not only prints the text with all
its orthographical confusions, abbreviations, and
alterations, but he also adds what he modestly
terms a restoration of the sonnet. Of this restoration I have made the subjoined version in rhyme,
though I frankly admit that the difficulties of the
text, as given in the rough by Signor de Tivoli,
seem to me insuperable, and that his readings,
though ingenious, cannot in my opinion be accepted
as absolutely certain. He himself describes the MS.
as a palimpsest, deliberately defaced by Michael

Angelo, from which the words originally written have to be recovered in many cases by a process of conjecture. That the style of the restoration is thoroughly Michael Angelesque, will be admitted by all students of Signor Guasti's edition. The only word I felt inclined to question, is *donne* in line 13, where I should have expected *donna*. But I am informed that about this word there is no doubt. The sonnet itself ranks among the less interesting and the least finished compositions of the poet's old age.

Thrice blest was I what time thy piercing dart
    I could withstand and conquer in days past :
    But now my breast with grief is overcast ;
    Against my will I weep, and suffer smart.
And if those shafts, aimed with so fierce an art,
    The mark of my frail bosom over-passed,
    Now canst thou take revenge with blows at last
    From those fair eyes which must consume my heart.
O Love, how many a net, how many a snare
    Shuns through long years the bird by fate malign,
    Only at last to die more piteously !
Thus love hath let me run as free as air,
    Ladies, through many a year, to make me pine
    In sad old age, and a worse death to die.

APPENDIX II

The following translations of a madrigal, a quatrain, and a stanza by Michael Angelo, may be worth insertion here for the additional light they throw upon some of the preceding sonnets—especially upon Sonnets I. and II. and Sonnets LXV.–LXXVII. In my version of the stanza I have followed Michelangelo the younger's readings.

DIALOGUE OF FLORENCE AND HER EXILES

Per molti, donna.

" Lady, for joy of lovers numberless
    Thou wast created fair as angels are.
    Sure God hath fallen asleep in heaven afar,
    When one man calls the bliss of many his !
    Give back to streaming eyes
    The daylight of thy face that seems to shun
    Those who must live defrauded of their bliss ! "
" Vex not your pure desire with tears and sighs :
    For he who robs you of my light, hath none.
    Dwelling in fear, sin hath no happiness ;
    Since amid those who love, their joy is less,
    Whose great desire great plenty still curtails,
    Than theirs who, poor, have hope that never fails."

THE SPEECH OF NIGHT

Caro m' è 'l sonno.

Sweet is my sleep, but more to be mere stone,
So long as ruin and dishonour reign ;
To bear nought, to feel nought, is my great gain ;
Then wake me not, speak in an undertone !

LAMENT FOR LIFE WASTED

Ohimè, ohimè !

Ah me ! Ah me ! whene'er I think
Of my past years, I find that none
Among those many years, alas, was mine ;
False hopes and longings vain have made me pine,
With tears, sighs, passions, fires upon life's brink.
Of mortal loves I have known every one.
Full well I feel it now ; lost and undone,
From truth and goodness banished far away,
I dwindle day by day.
Longer the shade, more short the sunbeams grow ;
While I am near to falling, faint and low.